C

MW01255072

Clear Vision

HOW 16 GROWING CHURCHES HARNESSED
THE POWER OF SHARED VISION

Jack Lynn

wesleyan
publishing
house

Indianapolis, Indiana

© 2005 by The Wesleyan Church. All rights reserved.
Published by Wesleyan Publishing House
Indianapolis, Indiana 46250
Printed in the United States of America

ISBN-13: 978-0-89827-293-2
ISBN-10: 0-89827-293-9

Editorial services by Julie-Allyson Ieron.

No part of this publication may be reproduced, stored in a retrieval system, or transmitted in any form or by any means—electronic, mechanical, photocopy, recording or any other—except for brief quotations in printed reviews, without the prior written permission of the publisher.

All Scripture quotations, unless otherwise indicated, are taken from the HOLY BIBLE, NEW INTERNATIONAL VERSION®. NIV®. Copyright 1973, 1978, 1984 by International Bible Society. Used by permission of Zondervan Publishing House. All Rights reserved.

CONTENTS

—⟋𝗆⟍—

INTRODUCTION

—◠◠◠—

S outheast Christian Church in Louisville, Kentucky, has a vision. And that vision has called them to take amazing leaps of faith over the years.

Imagine senior pastor Bob Russell telling his congregation (twice in eleven years): "We are going to have to relocate the church. We're getting ready to build a building with money we don't have for people we don't know."

Founded in 1962, Southeast Christian Church initially met at a school. By 1966 when Bob Russell was called as senior pastor, they were meeting in a house. Soon, Bob led them in a building program for a facility that seated 300. In April 1987 they moved a half mile to a new worship center that seated 2,500. Still the church continued to grow—and soon *out*grew—that new facility.

In 1992, just five years after dedicating the new worship center, Bob began to cast a vision for the church to relocate again. They considered options including intentionally splitting the church but eventually sensed the Lord directing them to remain together. In December 1998 the congregation relocated to its present site, a worship center that seats 9,300. They have since built an addition to the facility to accommodate continued growth. They now average 19,000 for weekend services.

What kind of a vision would cause a church to make these bold steps? Years ago the leadership of Southeast Christian Church established four key elements that would comprise their ministry vision:

- Evangelizing

- Edifying believers

- Ministering to those in need

- Serving as a conscience in the community

Leadership, staff, and congregation understand and live by that vision. It appears on their Web site, in their publications, in discussions at staff meetings, in planning meetings. They keep this idea in front of staff and congregation on a regular basis.

One of the ways they make these ministries practical is by having every staff member submit his or her top five goals each year. Those goals are reviewed by the leadership team, and staff members are held accountable to achieve them. If a staff member turns in goals that do not align with where the leadership of the church believes God is directing them to go, the staff members are asked to make appropriate adjustments.

The church also asks each member to commit to a minimum of one hour per week of Bible study, one hour per week of worship, and one hour per week of serving, all in the context of relational community.

The clarity of this vision has driven the people, staff, and lay leadership of this church to make heroic sacrifices to fulfill what they believe God has called them to do.

WHAT DOES THIS HAVE TO DO WITH ME?

At this point, you might be saying, "That's great for Southeast Christian Church, but what does it have to do with my church? What does it have to do with the business I run or the organization of which I am a member?" Those are valid questions, to be sure, and the remainder of this book is a response to them. The short answer, however, is this: a well-crafted, well-prayed-over, well-communicated vision will make all the difference in your ultimate effectiveness.

In the church we often assume everyone knows we simply need to be about the business of sharing the message of Christ with people who are far from God and building believers up in their faith. But there are many ways to accomplish those goals. God has chosen to prompt leaders to lead churches to express their ministries in many creative ways. It is significant for us to know where our local church fits into the mosaic God has so creatively placed in His body. We cannot assume all participants know what is expected, what their roles are, how we want things to be done, and what areas we sense God calling us to emphasize in our local expression of His body.

When churches bring clarity and intentionality to their vision and develop strong ownership of that vision in their people and leaders, they will see an amazing increase in the effectiveness of their ministry both inside and outside the church. This is not a new concept. In

The Next Generation Leader, Andy Stanley explains it as a difference between clarity and certainty.

> Uncertainty is a permanent part of the leadership landscape. It never goes away. Uncertainty is not an indication of poor leadership; it underscores the need for leadership.
>
> The art of clarity involves giving explicit and precise direction in spite of limited information and unpredictable outcomes. Imagine for a moment that you are the quarterback of a football team. It is fourth and eight. You are six points behind, and five minutes remain on the clock. What do you do? Kick or go for it?
>
> With limited information and facing an unpredictable outcome, you do what every quarterback in the situation does: You draw upon your knowledge and intuition and you call a play. You don't shrug your shoulders and send everyone to the line. You make a decision and send everybody into formation with specific instructions. And when the ball is snapped, you find out whether or not you made the right decision.
>
> In the realm of sports we see no conflict between uncertainty and clarity. We are accustomed to coaches, captains and catchers giving clear signals in

the midst of uncertainty. We have seen the chaos on the field that ensues on the playing field when the signal isn't clear. But in the worlds of business, politics, and ministry, uncertainty makes us uneasy. We hesitate. We become less specific and more general in our directives. Our people are unsure of what we expect. We yell "Hike!" and everyone runs in whatever direction he feels is best."[1]

The stakes are too high for us to wait until we have certainty in implementing the vision we have sensed the Lord has for us. We must be willing to give clear direction and clear leadership even when the results and pathways are not certain.

CREDIBLE, REAL-LIFE EXAMPLES

The chapters that follow are not simply built on one church's experiences. Rather, they flow from several lifetimes of ministry experience.

Of course, I draw from my own history. I have served for twenty-six years on the staff of Central Wesleyan Church in Holland, Michigan, under the leadership of Dr. Paul S. Hontz. I served as minister of music for seventeen years, as executive pastor for seven years, and as program director since August 2003. My current role involves overseeing age related ministries (children, students, young adults), overseeing the worship arts and technical teams, being the worship leader for the blended worship service on Sunday mornings, and serving on our management team.

But my own history in one church for twenty-six years is insufficient to draw conclusions for the wider church body. So, in the fall of 2002 I visited with leaders from vibrant, growing churches around the country. During those visits I asked a variety of questions about vision, strategy, mission, goals, and change; and I explored a variety of areas of ministry, asking what they do, why they do it, and how they do it.

Some of the ministry leaders in the study were from—

Saddleback Community Church	Lake Forest, California
Willow Creek Community Church	South Barrington, Illinois
The Chapel	Akron, Ohio
Germantown Baptist Church	Memphis, Tennessee
Bellevue Baptist Church	Memphis, Tennessee
Perimeter Church	Atlanta, Georgia
Cherry Hills Community Church	Denver, Colorado
Centenary United Methodist Church	Lexington, Kentucky
Ginghamsburg United Methodist Church	Tipp City, Ohio
Skyline Wesleyan Church	San Diego, California
Kentwood Community Church	Grand Rapids, Michigan
Southeast Christian Church	Louisville, Kentucky
First Assembly of God Church	Grand Rapids, Michigan
Cypress Wesleyan Church	Columbus, Ohio
Spring Lake Wesleyan Church	Spring Lake, Michigan
Colorado Community Church	Denver, Colorado

The leaders of these organizations were willing to share their journeys so others might benefit. I am grateful to them for their time and valuable input—and I know you will find their experiences relevant to your ministry.

So, I invite you to join me as we go to school on ministries that are seeing great success as a result of well-cast visions. As we see God at work in these ministries, we'll explore what clarity of vision might look like in your world. Perhaps the Lord will use this information to increase the effectiveness of your church or organization for further growing His kingdom.

PART ONE

VISION SHARING

CHAPTER ONE

THE POWER OF VISION SHARING

—ɯɯ—

> *The very essence of leadership is that you have to have*
> *vision. You can't blow an uncertain trumpet.*
> — Theodore M. Hesburgh

Suppose I asked you to meet me at a specific restaurant in your hometown Monday at noon. You would have all the information you need to fulfill that request: the time, the date, and the destination. How you reached that destination, though, would be up to you.

To get to the restaurant you might choose to travel through downtown. Or you might take the freeway to the nearest exit ramp. You could even take a third route weaving through side streets to avoid most of the traffic. It wouldn't matter to me how you got there. Once we agreed on where and when to meet, you would have the freedom to plan your own route.

Of course, there would be some *values* that would affect your decision. Budget limitations would prevent you from taking a helicopter. Ethical imperatives would deter you from driving 75 miles per hour through downtown. A moral code would prevent you from stealing a car to get there. Within the guidelines indicated by those values, you would be free to arrange the trip in whatever way seemed best to you.

Here is the point of application: an organization must clearly define both its *vision* and its *values* so that people will be empowered to enact the vision.

The vision of this chapter, for example, is that you'll understand how vision and values work together to help ministries fulfill Christ's mandate for them.

WHERE IS OUR FOCUS?

I believe there has never been a time that we need more focus than we need today. There are so many things calling for our attention, and the church is increasingly being viewed as irrelevant in our communities and world. George Barna says, "Since 1991, the adult population in the United States has grown by 15 percent. During that same period the number of adults who do *not* attend church has nearly doubled, rising from 39 million to 75 million—a 92 percent increase!"[1]

In today's culture there are demands of family, demands of work, demands of friends, and demands of other organizations. There is always the other church down the street that seems to have it all together. And there is always the megachurch that we can't compete with.

Yet, after much research I haven't found a compelling vision that is causing the people of today's church, particularly in North America, to be willing to make major life sacrifices to reach out into the world around us with the life-changing message of Jesus Christ. We are more concerned about style of worship, comfort of pews, climate-controlled air conditioning, and convenient parking than we are about setting and pursuing a compelling vision with great intensity and passion.

I must confess that I am often more concerned about my broken garage door opener than I am about making a sacrifice for Christ or taking a risk to reach out to someone in my sphere of influence who needs the hope of Jesus Christ in his life. Nevertheless, I'm not satisfied with this state of affairs—in my own life or in the greater church. So, I join many others in taking the position that says the local church is the hope of the world, and the world can be changed one life at a time. We must find ways to discover and focus on the ministry to which the Lord has called us.

What will it take to move us out of complacency and comfort? I believe a compelling, clearly articulated, culturally relevant vision that is effectively presented and modeled by leadership has the potential to make that difference. If this vision has been born in prayer, cultivated by the leadership of the church, and is biblically sound, it will move people to action.

Robert Lewis says this in *The Church of Irresistible Influence*:

More than by decades or centuries, history is marked by great ideas; that is, when someone, placed in a unique culture

and circumstance, stands up and says, What if we believed—
and acted upon—*this?*' Luther's idea of grace. Ghandi's idea
of nonviolent resistance. Ford's idea of efficiency. Hitler's
idea of nationalism. Eistein's idea of relativity. Jesus' idea of
the church. An idea is more than a starting point; in a deep
sense it is everything. An idea strong enough to spark imag-
ination, inspire sacrifice, build faith, and encourage perse-
verance is the most powerful human force on the planet. It
has the power to determine the future-for good and for bad.[2]

I believe each local church needs to have a driving "big idea" that
is unique to that local church, that local community, and unique to the
people and times of that local church. Dwight Robertson, president
and founder of Kingdom Building Ministries in Denver, Colorado,
says, "More time spent with fewer people equals greater results for
God." Implied in his statement is that we must be focused and not
just using a scattershot approach to ministry. We must focus like a
laser beam on the purpose for which God has created each one of us
and for which He has created our local church.

THE FREEDOM OF VISION

The burgeoning success of Rick Warren's best-selling book *The
Purpose Driven Life* and all of its related products is an indicator of
how deeply people feel the need for clarity of purpose in life. That
book and accompanying materials have sold millions of copies
because people are hungry for purpose and clarity in every aspect of

their lives—including their church lives. To make the most of this hunger, we need to get focused and become intentional about what God has called our local expression of His body to be and do.

At one of the churches I visited, I met with a member of the management team who expressed how they approach this issue: "We all go in whatever direction we feel will work for us. It has little to do with an overall sense of direction. We just do the best we can in our area of ministry and hope it will all come together in the end. Sometimes we end up crashing into each other because we didn't have an overall sense of direction, focus, and intentionality. We are all busy, working hard, and sincere about what we're doing, but there is little synergy and team. We're all doing our own thing."

I would contend that the people in this church could accomplish more, with greater satisfaction and less friction, if only they'd take the time to develop a clear vision. I say this because in my research I found that churches and organizations that function with vision are experiencing growth. They have a sense of freedom and purpose that motivates staff and lay leaders. They are willing to accept criticism about what they are doing and are even ready to take risks to do it. The result is that they are excelling in the vision to which God has called them.

THE FREEDOM OF VALUES

But a vision without underlying values leaves too much room for interpretation. Rather, a vision needs to be based upon a value system that is stated clearly for all participants. Remember our opening example? Our values kept us from some bad choices on the way to our destination.

Perhaps the values judgment isn't between right and wrong, but instead between good and best. Predetermined values can help us make these tough calls. Let's try this simplistic example to illustrate the point: Suppose your church has a stated value that says, "We believe excellence honors God." That value would keep you from putting up hand-written, sloppy signs on your doors. You would take the time to print them from your computer and mount them in attractive ways, the way excellence would require. This value also would keep you from winging it on a weekend service, without planning and rehearsing your sermon or creating an order of worship. Winging it on Sunday morning would be the opposite of excellence—and it would be contrary to the underlying values of your organization.

The freeing aspect of a value statement is that once everyone understands it, they can work in freedom without someone constantly telling them how to do things. That value would get built into the culture of how the church functions at every level.

WHAT'S YOUR DESTINATION?

It's great to create a vision and to determine its underlying values. But creation is simply not enough. Writing a vision statement and promptly filing it away will accomplish nothing. To be successful in motivating people to action, we need to state clear visions and then communicate them effectively to everyone involved—to fellow leaders, to ministry workers, and to those sitting in the pews.

Suppose I asked you if I could go for a ride with you in your car. Because you are a gracious person, you agree. As we get to the end of the driveway you ask, "Which way do I turn?" I respond, "Turn right." As we approach the next intersection you again look at me and ask, "Which way do I turn?" Again, I respond with a direction. As we approach the next traffic signal this exchange happens a third time. By this time I guarantee you will be frustrated because instead of telling you where we're going, I'll only give you a brief directive for the next turn.

Think of how freeing it would be if we had agreed on our destination before we left the parking lot. You would have known how to make those turns yourself. And both of us would have been at liberty to have a discussion about the subject of our choice because we would not have been bound by the need to give and receive directions at each intersection.

Yet, too often we do church by communicating to a select audience only a single turn instruction. We fail to agree upon a destination before starting our journey. So, we end up spending a lot of time making decisions at each intersection—wasting time and energy, and sapping enthusiasm from the most willing participants.

Here's a right-where-we-live example that I've seen happen on many occasions. A church hires a staff member to lead a youth ministry. The senior pastor has a picture of what success in youth ministry looks like to him: developing and reaching the students of families in the church. However, the youth pastor the church membership calls has a different vision. He wants to reach "street kids" who are on drugs, dress funny, and don't know proper church protocol. Are you beginning to see the major blow-up brewing here?

I saw a similar situation firsthand at a church where I served in my early days of ministry. The leadership was not prepared to have black students be part of the congregation. So, when we began to reach out to the local football team and some of the black students began to make a connection to the church, there was immediate resistance.

It would have been more effective for us to have worked through the issues ahead of time and establish a clear vision for reaching all people regardless of race. If that had been established and made clear, church members would have had the opportunity to understand and embrace that direction of ministry. However, since there was not a clear vision embraced and "owned" by the staff and lay leadership, there was confusion and frustration.

These kinds of misunderstandings can lead to difficult relationships, broken unity, and leaders that resort to micromanagement. Alternately, a clear vision defines the agreed upon destination. A clear vision paints that picture in a way that is easily embraced and understood by others, creating a pathway for negotiating the journey.

IS IT BIBLICAL?

Few could argue the fact that vision casting in secular settings—in the government or in the business world—is gaining measurable, positive results. But is vision really necessary in the church?

Some of you may say, "I know what church is about. We're supposed to win lost people and grow them into maturity in their faith. We're supposed to do worship services, missions, and some kind of stuff for children and students." Or you may say, "I just don't have time to develop a refined statement of purpose. I'm too busy meeting the demands of the people in my face every day. There are lots of needs around me, and I need to get busy meeting those needs not spending time in meetings coming up with fancy written statements." While both of these concerns deserve attention, they are insufficient excuses to avoid the rewarding step of determining vision.

As with all good questions, let's look to Scripture for some answers. I can think of at least three key biblical figures whose lives illustrate the power of vision to accomplish great things.

JESUS CHRIST

Who has ever lived a life more filled with purpose and focus than Jesus did? Listen to the words He spoke about His mission:

- "For I have come down from heaven not to do my will but to do the will of him who sent me. And this is the will of him who sent me, that I shall lose none of all that he has given me, but raise them up at the last day. For my Father's will is that everyone who looks to the Son and believes in him shall have eternal life, and I will raise him up at the last day" (John 6:38–40).

- Jesus replied, "Let us go somewhere else—to the nearby villages—so I can preach there also. That is why I have come" (Mark 1:38).

- He said to them: "It is not for you to know the times or dates the Father has set by his own authority. But you will receive power when the Holy Spirit comes on you; and you will be my witnesses in Jerusalem, and in all Judea and Samaria, and to the ends of the earth" (Acts 1:7–8).

In the first Scripture, Jesus said He had not come to do whatever came up, but rather He came to accomplish the specific will of His Father. That statement, alone, would seem to uproot the actions of the church I mentioned earlier whose management team lets individuals crash into each other rather than casting a clear vision for all to use as a guide.

In the second Scripture, there were things that had come up that were competing for Jesus' attention and time. He knew why He had come, and He was committed to staying focused on that purpose. So, He refused to be sidetracked or thwarted.

In the third Scripture, Jesus gave a clear and careful mandate to His followers. In due time, they understood His message and knew the role they had in carrying out the mission He had clearly articulated to them. The great part of this mandate that Jesus issued to His followers on that day is that it still can be our guide and direction for actions in our twenty-first century gatherings of Christ followers.

THE APOSTLE PAUL

Our example doesn't stop with Jesus' ascension back to His father. The Apostle Paul's ministry was known for its clear direction and vision as well. Note these two passages (although we could cite many more):

- I want to know Christ and the power of his resurrection and the fellowship of sharing in his sufferings, becoming like him in his death, and so, somehow, to attain to the resurrection from the dead. Not that I have already obtained all this, or have already been made perfect, but I press on to take hold of that for which Christ Jesus took hold of me. Brothers, I do not consider myself yet to have taken hold of it. But one thing I do: Forgetting what is behind and straining toward what is ahead, I press on toward the goal to win the prize for which God has called me heavenward in Christ Jesus (Phil. 3:10–14).

- After we had been there a number of days, a prophet named Agabus came down from Judea. Coming over to us, he took Paul's belt, tied his own hands and feet with it and said, "The Holy Spirit says, 'In this way the Jews of Jerusalem will bind the owner of this belt and will hand him over to the Gentiles.'" When we heard this, we and the people there pleaded with Paul not to go up to Jerusalem. Then Paul answered, "Why are you weeping and breaking my heart? I am ready not only to be bound, but also to die in Jerusalem for the name of the Lord Jesus." When he would not be dissuaded, we gave up and said, "The Lord's will be done" (Acts 21:10–14).

The Apostle Paul's vision was focused on becoming like Christ in every way. Everything he did in life and in ministry was inextricably tied to that goal. Even when others told him that His life was in danger, He did not allow himself to become distracted.

NEHEMIAH

The Old Testament is also replete with examples of men and women of vision accomplishing great things in God's strength. Consider Nehemiah, official in the court of the king of Persia. His life's work was turned upside down when he decided to sell out to the vision God burned into his heart.

For a brief refresher on how vision played a key role in Nehemiah's life, let's turn to a commentary on his life. This is how the book *All the Men in the Bible* describes Nehemiah's vision:

Nehemiah had a vision (Neh. 1). Nehemiah was deeply moved when he heard Jerusalem lay unwalled. For many days he mourned and prayed, deeply aware that this situation had been caused by his people's sins. Out of his awareness of the need and his immersion in prayer, Nehemiah developed the conviction that God's people, now returned to the holy land, must honor Him and rebuild the city walls. As the vision formed, Nehemiah realized that he himself had been called to carry it out.

Nehemiah committed himself to the vision (Neh. 2). Nehemiah held a key post in the administration of the Persian Empire and was a confidant of the king. Nevertheless he was ready to abandon his power and position to fulfill the vision. When Nehemiah asked the king for the governorship of the tiny district of Judah, his request was granted. This was a definite demotion as far as the world was concerned. But Nehemiah was committed to his vision of what must be done to honor the Lord.[3]

The fact that following God's vision was a demotion for Nehemiah is a powerful one to understand. And often there is a cost to submitting to a vision. It can cost individual independence, and it can require risk. But Scripture indicates that this passionate, yet risky, vision resulted in the betterment of the people of God. It caused the people to unite behind a purpose, to work toward a common goal, and to eventually see the city wall rebuilt (the vision accomplished).

These key Scriptures tell much of the story:

- "Then I prayed to the God of heaven, and I answered the king, 'If it pleases the king and if your servant has found favor in his sight, let him send me to the city in Judah where my fathers are buried so that I can rebuild it'" (Neh. 2:4–5).

- "When our enemies heard that we were aware of their plot and that God had frustrated it, we all returned to the wall, each to his own work. From that day on, half of my men did the work, while the other half were equipped with spears, shields, bows and armor. The officers posted themselves behind all the people of Judah who were building the wall. Those who carried materials did their work with one hand and held a weapon in the other, and each of the builders wore his sword at his side as he worked. But the man who sounded the trumpet stayed with me" (Neh. 4:15–18).

When Nehemiah stood before the king, he did not mince words. He knew exactly what to ask the king to do. His request was focused because the vision God was calling him to fulfill was focused. He then led the workers into a focused fulfilling of that vision in the face of great trials. Even when they were being threatened with attack, they kept their focus on the fulfillment of the vision by doing the work with one hand while holding onto a weapon with the other. They did not take their eyes off of the goal that was compellingly set before them.

WHERE WE LIVE

I submit to you that we must be equally focused if we are going to be successful in fulfilling the vision to which the Lord has called each of us and each of our churches. When we surrender to the immediate, to the urgent, and to the cares of this world, we lose the power that a focused vision can give us. As a result, we lose the powerful impact God has entrusted to us. We must be certain that we do not move to the latest and greatest just to be cool. We must be willing to change our strategies, our programs, and our methods for the single and solitary purpose of accomplishing the vision to which God has called us. We must be willing to let go of customs, traditions, programs, and methods that hinder us from achieving that vision—just as Jesus did.

Cypress Wesleyan Church in Columbus, Ohio, has established a clear vision that leaders articulated to all of their constituents. They determined that their ministry would be most effective at reaching "unconnected thirty- to forty-year-olds with children still living at home." They based this vision on the demographics of those they believe God has placed in their sphere of influence. Since this is their focus, they spend their efforts to plan programs to attract and hold this age group. What they don't do is spend a lot of time and effort to plan programs to attract people outside this target.

Their target has clear implications for children's ministry, student ministry, worship style choices etc. These are the details that work together to make the vision achievable.

Perhaps your church would not make a decision to create a target audience like Cypress Wesleyan and others have done. However, it is imperative that you create a clear picture of what you sense God has called your church to do and to be. Whether or not Cypress' specific direction applies to your situation, hearing about their vision will help you get a feel for the value of setting a clear vision for your ministry and communicating it clearly to all participants. If you do this, you will find your workers empowered in all areas: decision-making, strategic direction, and budgeting, to name a few.

DETAILS AND DESTINY

In the early 1960s President John F. Kennedy issued a clear vision for one area of the United States government. The mission was to explore space. The vision was, "We will put a man on the moon."

He even established a timetable. The values that underlay this vision were the subjects of safety, budget, and teamwork. It was amazing to see how this vision and its underlying values captured the American people, how it energized and motivated NASA employees, and how it impacted choices Congress would make for budgeting in the years to come.

What President Kennedy did *not* do himself was try to deal with how to accomplish this vision. He established firm values and left the how-to's for the scientists. He clearly stated what the picture of the future would look like, then allowed those more qualified than he to map out the minute-by-minute turns in the path.

Note that how-to's and details are important. But they are best left in the hands of those who know better than the leader how to accomplish the vision. Usually this knowledge falls to those working daily in the trenches.

In the church our vision is more critical than putting a man on the moon or sending people to explore Mars. If you are in leadership in your church, I have a series of questions for you. Please answer them prayerfully and honestly.

- Can you articulate the mission of your church?

- Can you articulate the vision?

- Can you articulate the values that drive your church?

- Are the people and the staff energized and motivated to join the team and move into the future with a reckless abandon for the ultimate cause of Jesus Christ that is being expressed through your local church?

- Do they have a clear picture of what you are calling them to do?

- Do they have a clear picture of how what they do fits into the overall direction of the church?

- Does someone have the responsibility to take the "big picture," break it down into more detail, and review applications of it for various departments and teams?

- Does your children's ministry team know how it applies to them?

- Does the team planning your worship services know how they apply this to the public worship?

- Do your board members know what kinds of questions are relevant at their meetings to make this vision take flesh?

Your answers to these questions will become more clear as you read on. Now let's turn our attention to the many different ways there are of doing church in the twenty-first century.

SEEING THE FUTURE

1. Take few minutes to pray, asking God to speak to you about what you have just read in this chapter. Are there things He wants to

speak to you about, things He wants to "burn into your heart," things He wants you to act upon?

2. Articulate the vision of your church or organization. Would others agree that that is the vision?

3. State how the role you have contributes to the fulfillment of that vision. Is your role clear? Does that role motivate you?

4. Can you articulate the primary values of your local church or organization. Write down the values that are well known within the organization. Are there any unstated values in your organization? List them.

CHAPTER TWO

HOW SIX CONGREGATIONS REDEFINED THE WAY THEY DO CHURCH

—∞—

> *Change is the law of life, and those who look only*
> *to the past or present are certain to miss the future.*
> —John F. Kennedy

It's Sunday morning and we get in the car, head to church, and arrive just in time (if not a few minutes late). We hustle to the sanctuary, sit in our favorite seats, nod hello to a couple of people, take a quick glance at the bulletin, and prepare ourselves to hear a welcome, sing, pray, give an offering, hear a message and head back home. Whew! We did our weekly duty of attending church. It makes us feel good about ourselves. It's one of the routines of our normal week. It's fairly predictable. We like predictability because change is painful and hard. There is enough change at home, at work, and in our community, and we just want things somewhere in life to remain the same. It seems church ought to be that place. After all, Scripture says, "Jesus Christ is the same yesterday, and today and forever" (Heb. 13:8).

Yet if we're going to be the compelling church that makes an eternal difference in our world, we will have to be willing to sacrifice some of the same old ways of doing things. We will have to—are you ready for this awful pronouncement?—*change*.

Germantown Baptist Church, just outside Memphis, Tenn., decided to no longer settle for the old description of who they were. So they made a conscious decision to move into a more impacting future, even if it meant making significant sacrifices and taking serious risks. As a result, over a two-year period, they saw 1500 people choose to move to other churches; however, during that same time they saw 2000 new people come to their church. Many were people who had gotten saved as a result of the church being more intentional, clear, and committed to reaching their community.

While this was a challenging time, it resulted in significant growth and impact for God's Kingdom. Sometimes we will have to pay a price or take risks to be the church God calls us to be.

THE NEED FOR RELEVANCY

Some may ask, "Why can't we just keep doing what we're doing?" I would reply that the stakes are too high to just keep doing what we've been doing. Charles Chaney, former vice president of the Southern Baptist Home Mission Board has said, "America will not be won to Christ by establishing more churches like the vast majority we now have."[1] Church researcher George Barna would appear to agree. Back in 1998 he said:

By the end of the decade, 50 million Americans will seek to have their spiritual experience solely through the Internet, rather than at a church; and upwards of 100 million Americans will rely upon the Internet to deliver some aspects of their religious experience.[2]

Even if Barna is only partly right in his assessment, we cannot help but change church—because people and technology make it impossible to continue as we are. Statistically, these several years after Barna's comments, we see a number of churches experiencing strong growth, but the overall picture of the church in North America is losing ground. If we keep doing what we've been doing, we will lose even more ground.

ASKING QUESTIONS

One of the criticisms Jesus regularly faced in His earthly ministry was that He was changing the way the religious people of that day were used to doing things. He was messing with the *status quo*. Likewise, John Wesley was criticized for preaching outdoors and not inside the walls of the church. Our forefathers were soundly criticized for using bar tunes with rewritten words as music in the church. Isaac Watts was nearly excommunicated when he introduced songs like "When I Survey the Wondrous Cross" and "I Sing The Mighty Power of God," because they were not verbatim Scripture. There is no place in the Bible that says we must meet at 11 a.m. on Sunday for corporate worship service that has a specific format and gets out at noon.

We must be willing to ask questions like: "Is what we're doing effectively reaching the world around us for the cause of Jesus Christ?" "Are we experiencing growth?" "If so, is it small incremental growth when God has plans for us that would enable us to experience exponential growth?" "Is our church biblically solid but culturally irrelevant?" We must never be willing to sacrifice being biblical to be relevant. The Scripture is the final authority of God, and in it is the truth that brings life and hope to our world. However, it is filled with story after story of God and His people doing things in unconventional ways. Think of Jonah, Joshua, Daniel, Paul, Peter, and Jesus. Many of the things that God moved these people to do were out of the norm.

AN EXAMPLE

For many years our local church has offered a Wednesday night high school ministry on our campus designed to reach out to the high school students of our church and community. For the last few years we consistently have seen 200 students regularly attend that ministry. Many students have come to know Christ; many have been called into vocational ministry and have seen God do amazing things in their lives.

But last summer we began to ask questions about what it would mean to reach out in a new way to a new set of people. Director of Student Ministries, Brian King, wrestled with the fact that we were not making enough of a difference in our community and challenged us to step it up. As a result we decided to take midweek high school ministry off campus into eight locations chosen for their proximities to local high schools. This approach resulted in significant changes that affected many families in the church. They had to deal with transportation issues, trust in new leaders, loss of central control for student ministry leadership, changes of schedules, and more. I am glad to share with you that this approach has been positively received by those within the congregation.

In our planning we determined that there are two pivotal questions that students will ask before choosing to come to something like this: (1) Will my friends be there? and (2) Do I connect with the leader? With these issues in mind, we began to pray and seek leaders for these communities — we would need eight missional pastors to lead the teams. God did some miraculous things to bring the right people into those positions.

The result? This year we have averaged 270 people in all of the communities — a 35 percent increase over a year ago. This result came because a group of people were willing to do ministry in a different way. They were willing to ask the hard questions and not be satisfied with what appeared to be success.

How They Do Church

While I was doing my research at the churches, parachurch organizations, and businesses on the subject of vision, I asked questions about the planning, staff training and development, goal setting, change management, policies and procedures, structures, mission statements, vision statements, style of leadership, frequency of major change, tools used in ministry, organizational structures, and culture of each organization.

I discovered that churches are doing church in many different ways. All of the churches I visited are evangelical, biblically grounded churches with the same mission as the church I serve: they all want to see lost people come into a personal relationship with Jesus Christ and fully mature in their faith. They all call for holy living, turning away from sin, and reaching out to be salt and light in their world. While the end goal is the same, methods differ vastly from organization to organization.

As I proceeded with the research and while compiling the results, it became increasingly clear to me is that it is not possible for each local church to be all things to all people. As a result many churches are getting more focused on the specific and clear vision the Lord has given them to fill in His overall Kingdom.

This is a change in the way they're doing church. It is difficult to generalize about how this focus and vision plays out in individual congregations, so perhaps the best way to illustrate is be for me to share a few specific examples.

COLORADO COMMUNITY CHURCH

Colorado Community Church (Denver, Colorado) has determined that God has called them to be "one church, many locations." They have launched two local expressions of their church, one in Aurora, Colorado, the other in Englewood, Colorado. They operate under one umbrella of leadership, but each campus is allowed to be unique in its ministry to meet the needs of its community. Three more campuses are planned for the Denver area. Each campus has its own senior pastor, but one senior pastor serves as lead pastor for the whole church.

Their motto is "We are not a place, but a mission." In accordance with this motto, they've adopted a "5 + 5" missions philosophy, which asks members to contribute a tithe of their income with 5 percent given to the local church and 5 percent given directly to the mission or ministry of their choice. This church makes the bold statement that they want to "grow fruit on other people's trees." They invite representatives from various missions and parachurch ministries to visit their church and set up displays. Then they challenge members to go shopping for the ministry that will receive their second 5 percent.

The different campuses collaborate on outreach ministries. For example, they have a clothes ministry and food bank in a common location, where they use standardized policies for distributing food and clothing. They also collaborate for the business functions of the church, for a receptionist, and for other infrastructure and common needs to keep from duplicating services.

Yet with all this collaboration, there is still room for unique local expressions of ministry. Each campus leadership team shapes local ministry to most effectively reach the community where their church is planted. This approach enables them to be more personal and more relevant, and to bear more fruit.

Lead pastor Robert Gelinas says the church desires to give entrepreneurial license to their people, empowering them to do the work of the ministry to which God has called each of them. He talks about equipping people to *be* a program and not just *do* a program. This church has a major focus on being laborers in the Kingdom and giving people a "Kingdom License." They place a high value on doing ministry in teams and not as lone rangers.

This approach to ministry has associated risks: How will you keep multiple campuses aligned with the same mission? How will you keep one senior pastor from going off in a different direction? If you give people entrepreneurial license, how do you know they won't come up with bizarre or inappropriate ministries that you cannot support or endorse?

Nevertheless, in the case of this church, the risks are paying off with a good return. Both campuses have impacted their communities and have been used by the Lord to reach people for Christ, minister to the poor, and make positive connections with marginalized people, while still being able to reach broad cross-sections of the Denver area.

NORTHCOAST CHURCH

The fascinating distinctive of Northcoast Church (Vista, California) is that the ministry offers five unique styles of worship at their weekend services, held on Saturday night and Sunday morning. This seems to work for the church, as it has seen attendance burgeon from 750 to 3,500 in eleven years.

Each of the five worship venues (all but one are on campus) has a live worship ministry including music, prayer, offering, and announcements. The teaching portion of the service, however, is presented live in one venue and seen via video in the others. The leadership says this approach has resolved the worship style preference issue for them.

Since each worship venue seats only 200 to 400 people, members experience the feel of a smaller church yet benefit from the ministries of a large congregation. They also benefit from a centralized infrastructure while allowing for individual worship expressions. They unite for children's ministry, student ministry, missions, and many other works.

The teaching ministry for the worship services utilizes a team teaching approach. The senior pastor is one of the primary teachers, but there are others who effectively teach the whole congregation regularly.

CYPRESS WESLEYAN CHURCH

Cypress Wesleyan Church (Columbus, Ohio) has geared its philosophy of ministry to a target audience. As I mentioned in the previous chapter, they aim to reach thirty- to forty-year-olds who have children living at home. Accordingly, they have narrowed their ministry wedge to be more effective in ministering to that demographic. All ministries are filtered through their we-can't-do-it-all philosophy. The older folks mentor younger families. Programs for children and teens receive high priority, and the worship music and style are geared for a thirtysomething and fortysomething audience.

This approach empowers decision making for lay leaders and hired staff who have a clear grid through which to sift ideas. For example, it would not fit the vision to buy a coach bus for senior adults to take on social trips. It would not fit the vision to build retirement homes on the property. It would not fit the vision to hire a senior adult pastor.

This clear focus of vision informs music selections for the worship leaders. It informs master planning leaders about facilities to plan for the future. It informs decisions about budget, staffing, and advertising.

How can a church focus on an age group like that? What about those of us who don't fit the focus? I am glad God hasn't called all churches to this model. However, He may have a specific group of people He wants to raise up through a focused ministry in Columbus that we are not able to fully see.

This vision has been born in prayer, and the leadership of that church senses that it is, in fact, God leading them in this direction.

BRENTWOOD BAPTIST CHURCH

Brentwood Baptist Church (Brentwood, Tenn.) started a Friday night service. Senior pastor Mike Glen explains, "We never could get the Saturday night thing to work. So we tried Friday night." This works for them because people get off work at 5:00 p.m., come to church at 6:00, then take their families out for dinner and have the rest of the weekend to be involved in other things.

This approach is consistent with the church's mission statement: "Connecting people to Jesus Christ through relationships, discipleship, and worship." The church determined to place a high value on relationships. This becomes a key to how the people go about reaching others in their community. The Friday night service helps facilitate the process of relationship building and reaching people who might not otherwise be reached.

PERIMETER CHURCH

Perimeter Church (Atlanta, Georgia) aims to reach metro-Atlanta by planting a series of churches—to date, they have twenty churches in that area and several more overseas. Each church becomes independent after being fully established by the mother church.

Perimeter Church added a staff person whose job is to share what they have learned with other churches. They have established a clear, focused vision that has been articulated in a book by senior pastor Randy Pope titled, *The Prevailing Church*. This has served as a guideline for the staff and the congregation to know the church's direction and philosophy of ministry.

The church's leaders make it understood that they cannot reach all of the people they would like to reach by having just one location. They seek to reach people from cradle to grave but have determined that their effectiveness will be enhanced by going to different parts of the Greater Atlanta area and planting local churches intentionally. This will allow each church to establish its own identity, strategy of reaching its community, and clear vision of how God wants to use it.

This is an intentional strategy for Perimeter Church and is not a series of "church splits" that occur because people are divided over issues.

WILLOW CREEK COMMUNITY CHURCH

Willow Creek Community Church (South Barrington, Illinois) has a well-established reputation as a church that focuses on reaching "seekers" and making their weekend services a tool for evangelism in the hands of their people. The weekend services are designed as a safe place to bring a person who is just checking out what it means to be a Christ follower.

A number of years ago, Bill Hybels, senior pastor at Willow Creek, bet the farm that it was right to build small-group ministry into the fiber of the church. They have invested thousands of dollars and thousands of hours in growing and developing this ministry. Small group ministry is also an integral part of helping people get connected and grow in their faith. Willow Creek has been willing to take great risks, trying many new and untested ways of reaching out into the unbelieving community, so that lost people can come to know Jesus Christ.

They are seeking to get everyone in the church into a weekend service, a small group, a place of service, and the midweek New Community service that is geared for believers' growth and nurture.

This approach is an intentional strategy and not just a trendy way to do church. The leadership is deeply committed to this strategic direction and is willing to take criticism from those who don't understand their approach and tend to think they are watering down the gospel of Jesus Christ.

Robert Schuller, speaking on a national television interview was asked, "What is the greatest challenge you face as a minister in your church?" His response was instant. "The greatest challenge I face is figuring out how to reach out to people outside the church without offending people inside the church."

PUTTING IT IN CONTEXT

These and many other examples demonstrate that there is not one right way to do church—or even two or three right ways to do church. Our Creator God has formed us in His image. That image includes creativity, and great creativity is evident in the many expressions of the body of Christ that exist today.

One of the key conclusions we can synthesize from hearing about such differing ways to achieve the same ultimate goal is that sometimes we will have to be willing to follow what we sense God has called us to even when it means that we must face challenges and criticism. God has integrally woven into His nature the whole idea of creativity. Many of these churches are finding creative and effective—yet challenging and new—ways of telling people about the great message of hope in Jesus Christ

I encourage you to consider what it means for you to evaluate the effectiveness of your ministries, ask hard questions, and deepen your commitment to greater impact and effectiveness, even if it means sacrifice and change.

After you've gone through this self-examination, you may find yourself and your ministry team asking, "What kinds of changes or shifts might we need to make?" We'll address that question next.

SEEING THE FUTURE

1. Take few minutes to pray, asking God to speak to you about what you have just read in this chapter. Are there things He wants to speak to you about, things He wants to "burn into your heart," things He wants you to act upon?

2. What are the distinctives of your church or organization that God is using to achieve the vision you have?

3. List some things that might need to change in order to achieve your vision? What is your attitude toward those changes? What is the attitude of others within your church or organization?

CHAPTER THREE

FOUR SHIFTS YOU MUST MAKE TO SURVIVE

—␖—

> *The past is a guidepost, not a hitching post.*
> —Thomas Holcroft

I promised we would talk next about the kinds of changes successful ministries and businesses are undertaking that you might also consider in your own sphere. Remember, even Jesus talked about the difficulty of expecting old wineskins to contain new wine. Change isn't easy—but it can be productive.

As I pursued my questions of successful organizations, I began to distill necessary shifts and changes into four broad categories. So let's turn our attention to these, one by one.

SHIFT ONE: SEE LESS AS MORE

Have you ever experienced a day like this? Get up. Shower. Meet with one of the committees of the church at 6:30 a.m. Go to the office and follow up on decisions made at that meeting. Review the upcoming Sunday services and make sure all the people involved are prepared for the weekend. Spend a little time preparing to preach or to teach a Sunday school class. Meet for lunch with a guy you are discipling. Come back to the office to return phone calls, answer e-mails, and review notes for the premarital counseling session you have in a few minutes. Meet with the couple. Make sure you have their wedding rehearsal and dinner as well as their wedding and reception on your calendar. Hustle off to your kid's soccer game. Make three calls on your cell phone en route. Contact the people heading the recovery ministry to encourage them. Place an encouraging phone call to the person heading the ALPHA ministry. Return a call from someone who was upset about the music last Sunday. Get home. Review your calendar for the next day, and realize you forgot to call the person who was concerned about the direction the youth ministry is taking. Remember that you never did get that material ready you promised to the people heading the prayer ministry.

Where in this day did you find time for God? Where did you find time for your own quiet reflection and listening to God? We often spend so much time trying to meet everyone's needs that we do not have time for the Father. We must come to the recognition that we cannot be all things to all people.

LISTENING TO GOD

I deeply believe a good work ethic is biblical. I want my kids to learn that I value hard work. However, I must be willing to carve out time for listening to God, for quiet reflection, for restoring my soul, for developing creativity. Life is not all about doing. I desperately need to make more time for being—if you're typical (and honest), you'll see this need in yourself as well.

Too often we measure our worth by how many hours we work, by how gifted we are at multitasking, by the quantity of our work, or by the length of our job descriptions. Yet the principle of less is more is something we also must value—for ourselves and for the people God has entrusted to our leadership.

For many years the traditional church asked people to come to Sunday morning worship, Sunday school, Sunday evening worship, and midweek prayer meeting, find two or three places of serving and attend the sweetheart banquet, the missions conference, the family life conference, the Bible conference, the women's conference, the men's conference, the couple's retreat, camp meeting, small group leadership training, and on and on. We tended to take the view that by attending and participating in all of these things, life change would happen, and we would become more like Christ. While it is a good thing to attend and participate in church events, we need to ask hard questions about the effectiveness of those things. Are they keeping us so busy doing that we haven't paid enough attention to being?

Jesus modeled attendance at the synagogue, as did Paul. However, when Jesus was asked to identify the most crucial elements in the Christian faith, He did not first talk about doing. He first talked about being. Consider His words, you shall "love the Lord your God with all your heart with all your soul and with all your strength and with all your mind" (Luke 10:27). Only after He voiced that first, greatest command, did He go on to say, you shall "love your neighbor as yourself" (Luke 10:27).

Activity does not necessarily mean achievement. Being busy doing the work of the church, attending the events of the church, and serving in the ministries of the church does not necessarily mean we are growing and becoming more like Christ.

DOING MORE WITH LESS

In my research I found that church after church highlighted the need to do fewer things with greater effectiveness. The senior pastor at Brentwood Baptist Church said, "We're going to do less better." Similarly, the executive pastor at Spring Lake Wesleyan Church said, "We have allowed the church to get so busy doing ministry that we have robbed the people of the gospel of peace."

Along the same lines, Southeast Christian Church has simplified its expectations for members by challenging people to invest a minimum of one hour per week in each of three activities: worship, learning, and service. They set manageable expectations for the amount of time they ask their people to commit.

In example after example, successful churches in this generation manage to avoid the trap of becoming so caught up in church work that they miss the point of what they are doing—winning lost people to Christ and helping them grow into fully devoted followers of Christ.

I'm not alone in this observation. Andy Stanley, in his book *Choosing to Cheat,* makes this startling but thought-provoking statement. Let me warn you, it may go against the grain of everything you've believed until now—but let me assure you, it is the truth:

If you stayed at work until everything was finished, . . . if you took advantage of every opportunity that came your way, . . . if you sought out every angle to maximize your abilities, improve your skills and advance your career . . . you would never go home. Likewise, if you stayed at home until every ounce of affection was poured out in all the appropriate places, . . . if you kept giving until every emotional need was met . . . you would never make it to work. So let me take some pressure off you. Your problem is not discipline. Your problem is not organization. . . .The problem is there is not enough time to get everything done that you are convinced— or others have convinced you—needs to get done. . . . There is just not enough time in your day to be all things to all people. You are going to have to cheat somewhere.[1]

I told you it would shock you. I'll bet Andy Stanley is the first pastor you've ever heard encouraging you to "cheat." And yet, it is a freeing concept. Yes, work hard. Yes, care deeply for your family. Yes, participate in church work. But know where to draw the boundary lines—when you've become so caught up in *doing* that you've ceased to *be*. Only then will you begin to see vision turn to reality.

There is a model for life that has appeared for years in various leadership training manuals. I learned the concept, called the Wedge, from Dr. Keith Drury. The essence of it is this: It is my job to go deep with God, and it is His job to manage the breadth of my influence. This is another way of addressing the issue of less is more.

THE WEDGE

Illustrated by this diagram, as I go deeper with God He allows the breadth of my influence to touch more people's lives for His purposes. When I start focusing on my breadth of influence, I lose the focus of going deep in Christ. I must keep my personal focus and priority right if God is going to be able to use me the way He wants.

I believe this principle is true in our personal lives, as well as in our ministries. God desires that we keep a narrow focus on the things to which He has called us; He will take care of the results and impact of our ministries. Because I believe this, I want to encourage you to consider the less is more idea for your personal life and for your ministry.

SHIFT TWO: MEET THE NEED

Well, that first shift might not have been too painful, but don't get comfy yet. We have some more to discuss. The next shift comes when we acknowledge the truth that we cannot be all things to all people. So we prayerfully determine the pressing needs around us, assess our available resources, and determine which of those needs God means us to meet.

Some churches are struggling to balance constituency needs and desires with available resources. At Central Wesleyan Church we have faced this challenge. A couple of years ago we laid out a set of priorities and gave the label "Mission Critical" to certain areas of ministry. We determined that to be effective in the future, we had to focus on making certain that children's ministry, student ministry, and Sunday morning worship services were all functioning effectively. This meant that we would focus on those ministries first. It also meant that other ministries, while important, would not get the same kind of attention and effort these would get. We came to believe that today's church must be effective in those "Mission Critical" areas, or it will not survive. Beyond that, each church will probably have other areas of focus that may change in emphasis over time.

As much as we would like to do so, we cannot give equal attention, budget, staffing, and time to every ministry. John Shaw, a friend from IBM, told me, "The recognition of a need does not constitute a call from God to meet that need." That is yet another freeing observation.

Likewise, Bill Hybels of Willow Creek Community Church acknowledges:

Christian leaders I have talked with who have faithfully worn the mantle of ministry for twenty, thirty, sometimes forty years, often attribute their longevity not to any particular things they did but to the many things they didn't do. ...

In recent years I've felt called to try to help other churches. So my addendum calling is to serve the Willow Creek

Association. But beyond that, my standard answer to most invitations is "No." I don't do executive dinners. I don't speak for corporations. I don't do men's retreats, marriage enrichment weekends, gospel cruises, or Holy Land trips. I respectfully decline all but a fraction of the opportunities that come my way. As politely as I can, I explain to those making requests what they are asking me to do is not in line with my primary calling. If I were to invest in what they're asking me to do I would have to take energy away from what God is asking me to do.[3]

As Mike McKay (a staff member at the church where I serve) and I met with Greg Hawkins, executive pastor at Willow Creek Community Church, we noticed that the whole church organization has become more selective in its ministry offerings. We were surprised to learn that they do not offer children's ministry during midweek services. They do not have a counseling center. They don't do major musical productions regularly. They are more focused, more specialized, in their approach to ministry. They have successfully made the shift from trying to meet every need broadly to focusing their efforts to meet a few needs well.

SHIFT THREE: DISCARD QUANTITY FOR QUALITY

That last observation leads us into the third shift in thinking we need to make in contemporary ministry—that of becoming more focused on quality than quantity. As we begin to think in these terms, it would help us to ask two key questions:

1. Is it possible that the success of our programs has become more valuable to us than changed lives? Spring Lake Wesleyan Church in Spring Lake, Michigan, made a decision to stop offering traditional Sunday school for adults, traditional Sunday night services, and traditional Christmas and Easter pageants. As they evaluated the impact of these ministries, they determined it would help the church become more effective to spend their collective energy in other areas.

2. Are almost all of our evaluation criteria based on numerical results? I remind you of the quote from Dwight Robertson, "More time spent with fewer people equals greater results for God." It is not only the quantity of our programs that matters. The qualitative impact of programs is perhaps more important. Empowering people to become personal living programs is a higher goal than amassing a number of mediocre ministries. Numbers are an indicator, but they are not an end in themselves. If we are producing life-changing quality in the ministries we offer, in most cases that will also result in increased numbers. However, it is possible to increase numbers without a significant qualitative impact on the lives of our people. The problem with doing numbers without quality is that we'll find that we're spending a lot of effort on what amounts to little (if any) eternal value.

The issue of quality came to a head at Central Wesleyan Church several years ago. For as long as anyone could remember, the Women's Missionary Society was the primary group responsible for championing the cause of world missions. Then the church, led by senior pastor Dr. Paul Hontz, formed the World Outreach Committee—to handle missions apart from the Women's Missionary Society. This necessitated letting go of some approaches to ministry that had been used for many years. Some even accused pastor Paul of being the guy who killed missions.

The cause of world missions is an A-list element of the church's mission. For many years the Women's Missionary Society was valuable as a means to an end. But it was *not* the main thing. The main thing was to be effective in reaching into the whole world with the gospel of Jesus Christ. In Central Wesleyan Church's reasoned evaluation, missions could be done better by replacing the old way with a fresh approach that would consolidate efforts and keep ministries from being spread too thin.

In the year this decision was made, Central Wesleyan Church had given $11,000 to world missions. The next year, because of the new approach, the church gave over $65,000 to world missions. Today nearly $1 million per year is going through Central Wesleyan Church to touch the world for Christ. In the 1990s the church sent about 100 people to full-time Christian service. Now, more than 1000 have been sent out on short-term missions teams. Letting go of the Women's Missionary Society was painful, but the fruit born since has proven that this was a right choice.

The clearer we make our vision, the easier it will be to focus on accomplishing more by doing less.

SHIFT FOUR: EVALUATE EFFECTIVENESS

If we're not going to take our measurements purely on the basis of numbers, then our next shift in approach will have to do with addressing just how we will evaluate ministry effectiveness.

Are you looking only through the eyes of your local church, or do you sometimes step back and look at ministry through Kingdom eyes? By this I mean, in the light of eternity—in the values of God's Kingdom—are the ministries of your church moving the greater cause of Christ forward? While we in our humanness tend toward building our own kingdoms, perhaps in the light of God's Kingdom we could partner with other likeminded churches in town to multiply our effectiveness. Perhaps we could partner with parachurch organizations or other agencies, and rather than duplicating ministries, we could strengthen each other—gaining more impact for our collective efforts.

After evaluating itself, Grand Rapids First Assembly of God prayerfully determined their vision to be a Spirit-filled, ethnically diverse, cell-driven church. Shifting to this focus required changes to programs that in the past appeared to be effective. Some of these changes included changing the church's name from "First Assembly of God" to "Grand Rapids First," refocusing the orchestra and choir, and freeing Sunday nights to allow time for cell groups to meet.

The time, effort, and energy being spent in many areas of ministry have been refocused to reach out into the community and seek to make a different kind of impact for the future. In the course of making these changes, they have had to develop more efficient ways to accomplish the ministry to which the Lord has called them.

ABCs of Focus

A few years ago Willow Creek Community Church went through an exercise that helped them set priorities for their church. They called it the ABC Bucket Exercise. First they listed every ministry in the church on separate cards, then they asked each person participating to place each card in one of three buckets. The A bucket was to hold the cards each person believed were mission critical, the cards representing ministries without which the church could not continue to be effective. The B bucket was to hold the cards each person believed were vital. The C bucket was to hold the cards that each person believed were important but not vital. This was a painful exercise, to be sure, because some good ministries needed to be shifted out of the main focus. But it was productive in that it allowed staff to make more vision-appropriate uses of their budget, time, and efforts.

Let me encourage you to do an honest inventory and quality analysis of your current ministries. Would you be open to asking the Lord to help you narrow down some of those ministries so that you might be more effective in the ministries that remain? To help you make this difficult but productive kind of evaluation of your own ministry, let me suggest some questions that you could use as a starting point:

- What would you cut out if your church had to do a 25 percent budget reduction? In the long term, what difference would it make?

- Are there ministries you are doing just because you always have? Are there any ministries you could stop and have few people even notice?

- Have you identified any fruit tests to the ministries you offer? Are they currently bearing the kind of fruit they once bore? Are you continuing ineffective programs because they were once effective?

- Are you continuing to use forms and methods that no longer meet the needs of the people?

Here are some practical things you could try to help sort through this idea. Gather eight or ten of the key leaders in your church (lay persons, staff members or both), and ask them to identify all the ministries your church currently offers. Make a list on a flip chart and hang the papers on the wall around the room. Next identify a set of criteria to measure effectiveness. This may include things like the following:

- Has anyone come to know Christ through this ministry in the last year?

- Has anyone new been added to this ministry in the last six months?

- Does this ministry actively help individual people to live out the fruit of the Spirit more effectively?

- Is this ministry growing numerically?

- Does this ministry regularly cause problems for the church? Are they good problems or bad problems?

- Does this ministry contribute to the unity of the church? Is it in any way divisive?

- Are the leaders of this ministry passionate about leading it?

- What would be the overall impact on the church if this ministry were to end?

• How broad or narrow is the impact of this ministry in our community?

Take this list of criteria and apply it to each of the ministries you listed on the flip charts. Then give each ministry a grade of A, B, or C. Put all of the A ministries in one list, all of the B ministries in another list, and all of the C ministries in a third list. I would suggest to you that the A ministries are the ones you must keep, change, adjust, and invest in. I would suggest the B ministries may be ones that need tweaking, attention, a small amount of investment, and more of a maintenance approach. The C ministries are probably ministries that you can let go. They are most likely not significant contributors to the overall effectiveness of ministry at your church.

DEFINING ANCHORS

Our final shift in thought has to do with the A ministries—those that anchor the work of God in your church or organization.

Another term we might use is the metaphor of a shopping mall. Every mall has anchor stores and specialty shops. Anchor stores carry the weight of the mall. They provide most of the traffic. They generate most of the interest. They generate most of the income. They draw the most attention. They also require the most space and resources. List all of the ministries you offer, then identify which ones are the anchor stores for your church. Again, those get the bulk of the energies and focus. Some specialty stores will be good to keep, but others may be thinning out the resources and need to be phased out.

Whichever way you choose to take a look at the ministries of your church I want to encourage you to sharpen your wedge, and let God drive you deep into Himself and the plans He has for you.

SEEING THE FUTURE

1. Take few minutes to pray, asking God to speak to you about what you have just read in this chapter. Are there things He wants to speak to you about, things He wants to "burn into your heart," things He wants you to act upon?

2. Review your calendar for the last thirty days. What general observations do you have about your use of time during that period? Do you see any evidence of "time abuse" that you need to address? Have you allowed yourself to get so busy doing church that you do not have peace in your life?

3. How much are you asking of the people in your church or organization? Are your expectations reasonable? Are they attainable? List some ways the less-is-more approach might be implemented in your situation?

4. To what extent do you evaluate fruitfulness in your church or ministry, and to what extent do you evaluate ministry based on numbers? Are there areas of your church or organization that were once fruitful but no longer are? If so, how might you address that situation?

CHAPTER FOUR

ESSENTIAL
CHARACTERITICS OF
EMPOWERING LEADERS

—⟶⟵—

> *Leaders establish the vision for the future and set the*
> *strategy for getting there; they cause change. They*
> *motivate and inspire others to go in the right direction*
> *and they, along with everyone else, sacrifice to get there.*
> —John Kotter

John Maxwell says, "Everything rises and falls on leadership." He is on the mark with the assertion that effective leadership is pivotal for your local church or organization to take the kind of clear-vision journey we've been describing to this point.

Perhaps you are one of the key leaders who will help lead your group on the journey. But, even yet, you may be saying, "Yes, I'm the leader. And all this makes sense. But I have no idea where to begin." That is an understandable response. Let's look next at the qualities of the leader him- or herself that will cause others to be motivated to follow. What does an effective, focused ministry leader look like?

PASSION

The first quality I think of when I consider effective leaders is their passion—their vibrant and enthusiastic pursuit of a vision that is so contagious that others can't help but join in on the journey.

I have seldom been around anyone as passionate as Dwight Robertson, founder and president of Kingdom Building Ministries in Denver. He is so zealous that when I am around him I often find myself wanting to leave what I am doing and join him. Each time this happens, I sincerely have to ask myself if I am being called by God to join Dwight or if I am simply being moved by the incredible passion God has given to him.

Because of his deep commitment, God has used Dwight and Kingdom Building Ministries to impact thousands of young adults and move them onto the playing field of life where they have become valuable, contributing laborers for God's eternal Kingdom. His passion captures and captivates them and gets them moving toward the vision of godly pursuits. Dwight's effectiveness, then, is wrapped up in his passion for a God-given mission.

PASSION FOR CHRIST

But he's not the only one to exhibit passion for Christ. Think back to an exchange between the Master and Peter on the night before Christ's crucifixion. As I describe the scene to you, try to picture the energy and passion of the man Peter for his Lord.

Jesus goes around the room, towel around His waist, bucket of water in His hand, washing the feet of one disciple after the next.

Then He comes to Peter. The others have been silent, but Peter's passionate nature causes him to blurt out, "Lord, are *You* going to wash *my* feet?"

Jesus replies, "You do not realize now what I am doing, but later you will understand."

"No," said Peter, "You shall never wash my feet."

Jesus answers, "Unless I wash you, you have no part with me."

"Then Lord," Simon Peter replies, "not just my feet but my hands and my head as well."

That's passion. That's all-or-nothing selling out to God. And that's contagious.

To affect change in an organization and in lives for Christ's kingdom, there must be a deep passionate desire within the leader to discover and develop the vision that comes from the Lord. This will cause the leader to "stay by the stuff" even when the journey gets challenging and difficult.

WELL-PLACED PASSION

The knowledge that the Lord himself has called you to this journey will keep you motivated to move forward against obstacles, while a shallow desire to be involved in the latest buzz of the church world will do little to sustain you in times of difficulty. I have seen many people attempt to launch ministries or change existing ministries because they went away to a conference and heard a great story about how God did a powerful work in another place by using an innovative approach to ministry. I have seen many of those ministries fall flat because the leader didn't have the depth of passion for the real purpose and focus of that unique ministry. Instead, he got caught up in the newest idea.

At times our creativity can become an end instead of a means. We must always know what the prize is and then keep our eye on that prize. The prize never changes. The methods for achieving the prize may change often. Let's make sure we don't get those two things mixed up.

Leader, do you feel great and deep passion for what you sense God has called you to lead? Do you communicate that passion by your words, your actions, and your attitudes?

OPENNESS AND VULNERABILITY

The next key quality of an effective leader is the ability to be transparent, to be real and vulnerable to those under his or her leadership. An unapproachable leader will not motivate people to follow through winding paths. Perhaps that is why Christ called himself our Shepherd—a hands-on leader who is very present with His flock and who made himself vulnerable to the point of laying down His life for His sheep.

The Apostle Paul, one of the greatest leaders and influencers of the early church made this statement in his letter to his friends and converts at Corinth:

When I came to you, brothers, I did not come with eloquence or superior wisdom as I proclaimed to you the testimony about

God. For I resolved to know nothing while I was with you except Jesus Christ and him crucified. I came to you in weakness and fear, and with much trembling. My message and my preaching were not with wise and persuasive words, but with a demonstration of the Spirit's power, so that your faith might not rest on men's wisdom, but on God's power. (1 Cor. 2:1–5)

Paul obviously felt the freedom to disclose his own sense of weakness and fear early in his time with the Corinthian believers. It is interesting that he would remind them of this vulnerability early in a letter where he would have some pretty tough things to say to them. It is as if he is reminding them that his openness with them earned him the right to have their own vulnerabilities laid bare before him. Clearly, his openness served to strengthen his already strong leadership role among these believers.

In our day, this kind of vulnerability can be seen when leaders are honest about their own struggles and failures. Dan Seaborn, president of Winning At Home (an organization that exists to help build godly families), tells this story about one of his own failures:

I was performing a wedding for a young girl in the church where I had served, and my wife, Jane, and I were both dressed up. At the end of the wedding, I told my wife I wanted to take her out to a nice place to eat for dinner with just the two of us. Jane wanted to stay and visit with the people she knew who were attending the wedding. Finally, though, she did agree to leave and go out for dinner.

When we got in the car, I said to Jane, "You don't look like you want to do this." She responded by saying, "Just give me a minute, and I will be okay." I didn't like that. I wanted her to be glad that we were going out with just the two of us.

We got into a pretty heated discussion, and Jane decided to move to the backseat. I continued to talk to Jane by adjusting the mirror so I could see her. Dripping with sarcasm, I said, "This is going to be really good. People who know us and see us riding down the road like this will think this is really cool." Finally I asked, "What are you doing?"

She responded, "I have been thinking about the last fifteen minutes and what just transpired and have been asking the Lord to show me what I have done wrong." That led to a discussion where I apologized and told Jane I loved her.

The story has a happy ending because we ended up making up, eating at Applebee's, and playing footsie under the table during dinner. Years ago this would have been a three-day fight. However, the Lord has helped us to grow and be able to deal with things like this in a much healthier way.

I find it ironic that the person leading a major organization to build godly homes tells this story about himself where he initially failed. But the beauty of this story's vulnerability is that is helps me identify with Dan and know that he wrestles with some of the same things I wrestle with. His vulnerability with audiences causes people to listen even better when he challenges them to improve their marriages.

Almost everyone appreciates and values it when leaders share with the key people around them the deep and significant things in their lives. Sometimes we tend to think that sharing our weaknesses will cause others to view us as weak or incapable. On the contrary, they will view us as real, approachable people who have similar issues to deal with as they do. It encourages them to pray, to support, and to build a spiritual bond with us.

This kind of openness also opens the door for leaders to invite accountability into their lives, which is another key biblical concept. We don't have to look far to find leaders who have resisted accountability and vulnerability and lost the ministry which the Lord had entrusted to them. When we are open and honest with a few key people around us it allows the Holy Spirit to use them to help make us more like Christ. We can be both a giver and a receiver of ministry.

ANOTHER EXAMPLE

A few years ago Dr. Ron Cline, then president of HCJB Radio, was a guest speaker at my home church. While there, he told a story of arriving at the San Francisco airport on a flight that had been delayed. He rushed to catch his connecting flight and discovered that the plane was still at the gate but the door had been closed. It was going to be two hours before he could catch another flight. The ticket agent would not allow him to board the plane even though it was still sitting at the gate. He found himself feeling frustration and hostility.

Then God began to speak to him about his attitude. God asked him questions like, "Do you think you know better than I where you need to be and when?" "Do you think you know your needs better than I do?" "Do you think you know what is best for you better than I know?" As he began to listen to the Lord, he made a decision to change his attitude and use the time for some constructive purpose.

He had just received a temperament test that used selection of colors to help identify a person's temperament. However, he discovered he did not have a pencil with him. He walked up to the counter and in a frustrated tone asked the ticket agent, with a frustrated voice, if he could borrow a pencil. She told him he could but that he would have to use it at the counter. He spread out the pages of the test and began to mark the appropriate pages. As he did so, he began to tally the results of the test and observed that the test was identifying a significant level of hostility. He laughed as he recognized the irony of the situation.

The ticket agent asked what he was doing, and he explained it to her. She asked if she could take the test. He gave her the test and shared that it revealed that she was feeling fearful about something. She said that was true and asked if he had time to talk.

He responded by saying that he had two hours. They went to a meeting room where Ron was able to talk with her and lead her to faith in Jesus Christ.

As he was telling this story, I identified with that struggle. I had recently been on a flight where I had been delayed, my luggage had been lost, and I also became irritable. Ron's willingness to share that story of his weakness and frailty helped us identify with him even as he spoke to us and challenged us to surrender our lives to Christ. His vulnerability caused the message to take flesh.

MY OPPORTUNITY TO BE VULNERABLE

It wasn't much later that I had my own opportunity to be vulnerable with someone in my organization.

I recently had a lady apologize to me for missing an event she was scheduled to be involved in. She came with a genuine sense of regret. She apologized and told me she had simply forgotten.

I responded, "Apology accepted. I'd love to be able to yell at you for missing this important event because that has never happened to me. However, I know exactly how you feel, because I've blown it like this too."

She responded by laughing and acknowledging that she appreciated my understanding. She was also on time at the next event a few days later. The fact that I admitted my failures in the past did not cause her to lose respect for me. In fact, she appreciated and valued the understanding and deepened her commitment not to make that mistake again.

This kind of vulnerability and openness does not include sharing inappropriate and confidential things. It simply means we share with an honest and open heart the joys, the hurts, the weaknesses, the temptations, the issues of our lives, and then invite others to join us in the journey of a growing faith. Sometimes we leaders can come across as having our lives so together that others can't imagine how they could live at the same level. Rather than thinking, *If they only knew,* let's tell them. Let's be open, real, and vulnerable in appropriate and gracious ways. This will create an atmosphere that is healthy and contagious and will cause those around us to feel even more a part of the team. It will take that kind of leadership to lead the people through the kind of change that enables them to have a laser-like focus on the ministry to which God has called you.

WHAT VULNERABILITY IS NOT

There is a difference between open vulnerability and uncertainty. Let me illustrate. Suppose you are preparing to lead a board meeting, and the major issue on the agenda is whether or not to ask a staff member to leave the staff of the church. A person with little vulnerability would come to the board and say, "I believe we need to let this person go. I know it will be hard on some, but it's just the right thing to do." This sounds like a person who "has it all together" and will not tolerate anyone else who does not "have it all together."

A person with uncertainty would come to the table and allow unguided conversation about the issue without establishing ground rules or direction. "I don't know what to do about this," he would begin. "You talk it out and decide. I'll go along with whatever you say."

Neither of these styles exhibits good leadership.

However, a person with a spirit of openness and vulnerability who is giving clear leadership might say, "I have wrestled with this issue long and hard and my spirit is grieved. This person is my friend, and I have cried more tears over this than you can imagine. However, my sense is that we should let this person go. I believe that is the right thing to do. I know I am close to the situation and may not see things clearly. Sometimes my judgment is flawed when I'm this close to a situation. I need the valuable input you as board members will give to help sort through this. I stand in need of your support and help."

Those board members in the first scenario will feel like they are being railroaded. Those in the second will feel like they are not being led and that all the weight of the decision is on them. In the third scenario, though, they will feel like you value them, you care about them, and you are not invincible. However, they will also feel like you have led them by giving them your view of what should happen. On their way home that night in the car they may make comments like, "I am thankful our pastor is willing to let us see his humanness. I appreciate his leadership."

Does this mean that you cannot stand strongly for what you believe? Absolutely not! It simply means that there is a spirit of humility and grace that is expressed because of being open with your own fears and concerns.

INCREASING YOUR EFFECTIVENESS

If you want to increase your effectiveness in the area of vulnerability, here is an exercise you might try. Ask the people closest to you on your staff, on the board, or in other leadership roles to score you on the following questions with 1 being low and 5 being high:

- I would describe _____ as being open and vulnerable.

- I know _____ struggles with some of the same issues I struggle with.

- _____ frequently expresses appropriate emotion.

- _____ does not come across as "having it all together."

After getting this feedback, read and evaluate how they see you on this vulnerability issue. It may be beneficial to have a roundtable discussion with them and ask them to help you open up more if you desire to do that.

Above all, though, if you are feeling led to move your organization toward a clear vision, I would challenge you to be in prayer, asking the Lord to equip you with the passionate enthusiasm for the vision and appropriate personal vulnerability that it will take to cause others to come along on the journey with you—and stay with you until it reaches its apex.

TURNING A CORNER

Until this point, we've been focusing our attention on creating the vision and sharing it with those in our spheres of influence. Without these early steps, no vision can be fulfilled. However, in themselves, they are insufficient—for they only get us started. There is much more to seeing clear vision through to its completion. I call the next step "vision enabling." And that's where we'll turn our attention in the second section of this book.

SEEING THE FUTURE

1. Take few minutes to pray, asking God to speak to you about what you have just read in this chapter. Are there things He wants to speak to you about, things He wants to "burn into your heart," things He wants you to act upon?

2. What are you passionate about?

3. Name one area in which your need to increase the effectiveness of your leadership.

4. Describe your level of openness and vulnerability to those around you. Would others agree with your assessment? Consider asking them.

5. What accountability measures do you have in your life? How effective are they? If changes are needed in this area, how and when will you make them?

PART TWO

VISION ENABLING

CHAPTER FIVE

ENABLING VISION BY PRAYING TOGETHER

—ᴍ—

> *Give to us clear vision that we may know where*
> *to stand and what to stand for.*
> — Peter Marshall

What is it about prayer that packs such a powerful punch? I recently read a saying by an anonymous author that might shed some light on this question, "When we work, we work. When we pray, God works." If all of the plans we put together are only a result of our thinking, our ingenuity, and the thinking of a committee or board, they will amount to nothing of eternal value. The Scripture says, "Unless the LORD builds the house, its builders labor in vain" (Ps. 127:1).

Yet, for all its power, consistent prayer can be as difficult to motivate ourselves and our congregations to practice as personal evangelism is. Satan fights the two Christian disciplines of evangelism and prayer harder than almost anything else. I believe more Christians walk around on a day-to-day basis with a greater sense of defeat about prayer and evangelism than anything else in their relationships with Christ.

Nevertheless, if we are going to be about the ministry the Lord has called us to be about, we will have to address these two issues. For the purposes of this book, I am going to focus on the great need for a prayer movement within the local church.

The clear vision I am challenging you to develop for your ministry must be born in prayer. If this vision does not come from the heart of God, it will not bear spiritual, lasting, eternal fruit. We can find the heart of God by focusing our energies on two primary tasks: reading and studying His Word and spending time with Him in prayer, both talking and listening.

It is not enough for us to have churches and organizations that pray. We must build praying churches and praying organizations. Instead of just the cursory opening prayer we often have in our meetings, we must have times of deep and meaningful prayer. Instead of brief times of prayer as we cut in and out of traffic, we must find times—on a consistent basis—for deep and meaningful prayer.

JESUS' PRAYER LIFE

When Jesus was about to make major decisions about His ministry, He spent all night in prayer. Listen to the way Luke describes one key instance of the connection between Jesus' prayer life and His actions: "One of those days Jesus went out to a mountainside to pray, and spent the night praying to God. When morning came, he called his disciples to him and chose twelve of them, whom he also designated apostles" (Luke 6:12–13).

In other places in Scripture we find similarly challenging statements about Jesus' prayer life:

- "Very early in the morning, while it was still dark, Jesus got up, left the house and went off to a solitary place, where he prayed" (Mark 1:35).

- "But Jesus often withdrew to lonely places and prayed" (Luke 5:16).

- "When he rose from prayer and went back to the disciples, he found them asleep, exhausted from sorrow. 'Why are you sleeping?' he asked them. 'Get up and pray so that you will not fall into temptation'" (Luke 22:45–46).

Even though Jesus was the Son of God, He still felt the need to spend significant amounts of time with His Father in prayer before launching into each step of His ministry. He bathed major decisions in great amounts of prayer.

I believe this is a model not only for how we should approach the development of a clear vision but for how we can see that vision past the initial launch and all the way to completion. After all, Jesus prayed throughout His years of ministry, not just at the beginning.

Prayer-Driven Ministries

While on my sabbatical, I discovered what some churches are doing to try and build the practices of prayer into the fabric of their ministry. Most begin with establishing a measurable, concrete core value of prayer at the staff and committee level—knowing that as go the leaders, so go the people. Perhaps the stories of how prayer integrates seamlessly into the fabric of these leadership teams, committees, and congregations will begin to spark ideas that you can apply prayerfully to your own situation.

Kentwood Community Church

Kentwood Community Church in Grand Rapids, Michigan, has this among its core values: "We believe that God desires our prayers, and God's house is to be a house of prayer. Jesus taught us how to pray and demonstrated the power of prayer. Prayer is two way communication with the Almighty God." Staff members are asked to report on their prayer life as part of their regular staff evaluations.

Senior Pastor Wayne Schmidt says that each week in public worship services they ask for prayer requests from the congregation and typically receive 100–150 requests. Each staff member is assigned to a portion of those requests. He will pray for that need and then send the person a note letting them know the staff prayed for him or her. They also take prayer requests in staff meetings by dividing into groups of three and asking for other requests from fellow staff members. This keeps prayer in front of the leadership team on a consistent basis and helps to make the annual performance review question about prayer more relevant.

CENTENARY UNITED METHODIST CHURCH

At Centenary United Methodist Church in Lexington, Kentucky, every vision team has a prayer secretary who tracks and reports on prayer requests and answers to prayer within its group. To reinforce the reason for this task, the church includes the following statement in its staff covenant: "Guided and empowered by the Holy Spirit, we covenant to be purposeful and fruitful in our ministries, accountable to and praying for one another."

SPRING LAKE WESLEYAN CHURCH

Spring Lake Wesleyan Church in Spring Lake, Michigan, states this core value for its staff: "We are a team that is driven by prayer. Prayer is the source of ultimate guidance, power, affirmation, and fellowship. God accomplishes more than we could ever dream." The church's vision statement includes the following:

We have a dream of a contagious community of believers who actively seek and find God in prayer. Talking with God is becoming as normal as talking with a close friend. Prayer alone, with fellow believers, and even with those who don't yet know God personally, are common. Times of prayer serve as the power behind the ministry effectiveness of this church.

The operational value statement for the staff at Spring Lake declares, "We have a value of being prayer immersed." I like the phrase "prayer immersed" because it paints a picture of going into the depths of prayer—not just skimming the surface. To live out their value statement, Spring Lake leaders ask three questions of every new ministry, program, or idea: Have we prayed about this? How have we prayed about this? How long have we prayed about this? That's prayer immersion.

BROOKLYN TABERNACLE

Because of the best-selling books Pastor Jim Cymbala of the Brooklyn Tabernacle has written, many may be aware of the emphasis that his congregation places upon prayer. But not only have I read what he has written about prayer, I've seen it firsthand.

In June 2003 I visited Brooklyn Tabernacle's Tuesday evening prayer service for the third time. That night, I had a fascinating conversation with a parishioner who sat beside me. "Hi, Ma'am! I am visiting from out of town and wondered if it would be okay to ask you a couple of questions." She responded with an open invitation to talk. I asked if she had worked all day. She said she lived in Brooklyn but had worked all day in Manhattan—at best, a forty-five-minute subway ride. I asked if she had been home since leaving for work that morning, and she indicated that she had not. I then asked, "What makes it worth it for you to leave home early in the morning, work hard all day, skip dinner, and come to the prayer meeting at Brooklyn Tabernacle for about two hours?"

She looked at me like I was from another planet. She turned to face me and said, "I can hardly imagine how I would make it through my week if I did not take time to come to the house of the Lord, worship Him, and pray with the other believers in this place. This time of prayer is so powerful in my life, I can hardly imagine not being here. I come here tired, but I leave full of the Holy Spirit and filled with His power. God uses this time of prayer to meet me where I am and hear my love for Him as well as hear the cries of my heart."

I was moved and convicted with how little I sensed that desperateness in my life for prayer.

But it isn't just the parishioners in the pews who have woven prayer into the fabric of their lives. That evening I watched as they invited all the pastoral staff of the church to come down front. Then they invited all the children, middle school, and high school students, as well as all the college students to come forward and go through a line where one of the pastors laid hands on them one-by-one and prayed for the students as they faced the summer in New York City. They prayed that God would protect them on the playgrounds, protect them in the housing projects, provide jobs for the older ones, and use them in ministry to reach out to others. This was not a three-minute prayer of blessing. The process probably took thirty or forty minutes. It was rich and filled with power and meaning. I was moved by this meaningful investment of prayer in the lives of their children and students. Clearly, this is a praying church, not just a church that prays.

The leaders of Brooklyn Tabernacle have decided that they cannot do the ministry to which God has called them apart from deep and meaningful prayer—and they have communicated that passion to all their staff and all their parishioners.

INCREASING THE EFFECTIVENESS OF PRAYER MINISTRY

As you seek to make prayer deep and meaningful for your congregation, I'd encourage you to survey your people (allowing them to remain anonymous). Ask questions about how often they pray, how long they pray, and the top five concerns they pray about most frequently. My experience in taking such a step suggests you will discover insights that may be helpful to you in planning teaching/preaching ministries on many subjects, including the subject of prayer. You could provide training resources for this team by recommending books, tapes, CDs, videos, DVDs, seminars, workshops, and conferences. Later, when the whole congregation becomes involved, these resources could be shared with all who are interested.

Next, I'd recommend that in tandem with your personal and staff prayers, you gather and develop a team of strong intercessory prayer warriors from within the congregation or organization—those whose spiritual gifts and personal commitment to prayer show evidence that God has gifted them as intercessors. Ask this team to pray that God would help the church become a house of prayer. The people who are gifted as intercessory prayer warriors will love being challenged to this ministry. No one will be more passionate for making prayer a high value at your church.

Not only do you want your own work to be bathed in prayer with these prayer warriors, but having every staff member recruit and meet regularly with a group of prayer partners is a way of extending and expanding the breadth of prayer's reach within the group. Perhaps you might even ask every board member to form a prayer partner team. This also reinforces the value of prayer and places a heightened awareness on the board members that they need prayer as they make decisions about the ministries and future of the church. It puts them in a place of dependence on the Lord.

After you have laid a strong foundation, it will be time to involve the entire congregation or group. One way to begin this process is to open meetings with seasons of prayer instead of a more typical opening prayer. You'll need to take time to create a plan if you intend to have an intentional, extended time of prayer. Your plan could include asking people to pray Scripture related to the subject of the meeting. It could include conversational prayer. You may want to structure a prayer time that includes confession, listening to God, intercession, and praise. Some of this time may allow for praying silently as individuals, some for small groups, and some for the whole group.

Another way is to take time in the services to have meaningful in-depth prayer and not just a pastoral prayer. Prayer so often becomes a performance of the pastor for the people. Facilitating the people's active participation in prayer could involve opening the altar for people to come to during the service. Or it could involve a time of directed prayer where the leader suggests prayer specific concerns and allows times of silence, giving the people time to pray about the things that have been suggested.

Likewise, as prayer begins to play this integral role, you'll want to be sure to pay attention to the issue of answered prayer. Perhaps you'll want to make time in certain services to share testimonies about answered prayer. This will allow others to be encouraged by seeing the work of God on display. When we share valid, legitimate answers to prayer, it puts the work of God on display for His glory and for our edification and growth. When we talk about prayer answers then follow up by asking people to pray that God would guide us to a clear picture of what He wants to be about, people will see that God can and will guide us into His vision for us. In short, answered prayer in the past is a faith builder for answered prayer in the future.

Here are a few other options for ways to enhance the prayer life of your entire group:

- Set aside an evening of prayer, or plan a prayer retreat. Make this a time of doing prayer, rather than just talking about it. Be creative in how you encourage and equip people to pray during these times.

- Identify and publicize times that the worship center will be open to everyone for private prayer at the altar.

- Form teams of people to do an annual home visit to all of the families in the church, asking for their prayer needs and praying with them. Give a summary of these prayer requests to the team of intercessory prayer warriors. Make the requests available at staff and board meetings. Not only will the prayers avail much, but the information will help your leaders understand the issues that people of the church are facing.

- Ask every committee to have a prayer secretary and record prayer requests and answers to prayer just as they would record meeting minutes. Make sure the prayer report gets included in the minutes and is forwarded to the team of intercessory prayer warriors.

- Network with other organizations such as Moms in Touch or National Day of Prayer.

- Create a prayer chain that works by phone and e-mail for immediate needs.

DEVELOPING A PRAYER MINISTRY

Some overall principles that will help guide the development of prayer are to include times of confession, praise, thanksgiving, and intercession. This will allow for a balanced prayer time, rather than just listing off a litany of requests.

Another principle is to pray specific Scripture for specific needs. I often pray Philippians 4:6–7 and Isaiah 26:3 for myself when I am facing anxious times. I also pray James 1:5 for myself when I am needing the wisdom of the Lord. Many times I pray that my children would live out Matthew 22:37–39, the greatest commandment. At times when my trust is wavering or someone I am with needs a word of encouragement about trust, I pray Psalm 20:7.

Finally, challenge leaders to model a commitment to faithful prayer. Ask for a written commitment. Ask them how they're doing on a regular basis. Ask yourself if you are leading the way with your own prayer practices. We will seldom hold others accountable to what we are not practicing ourselves.

A CHURCH DEFINED BY PRAYER

The setting is New England. It's not the middle of the Bible belt or a place many would expect to see a great work of God happening; however, a great work of God is happening at Presque Isle Wesleyan Church in Presque Isle, Maine. I had the opportunity to learn more about the story of this church and to learn more about the work God is doing there when I talked with pastor Rick Kavanaugh.

Rick came to pastor there in 1986 when attendance was about 130. He had a fairly typical pastoral experience for six years—things were okay but the church was not seeing significant strides in growth or development. This was a church that was friendly and gracious; people treated each other like family. Yet they were not making any major inroads in reaching the community with the message of Jesus Christ.

By 1992 the church was just over 100 people, and pastor Rick felt he needed to resign and move on. After he resigned, though, Rick sensed the Lord "check his spirit" and felt the Lord telling him to go and see if he could "unresign." In obedience to the Lord he did that, and the people graciously accepted his return.

Soon after that he attended a center for pastors who are burned out. He wanted to learn to counsel others and was, in fact, counseled himself. This launched him into a prayer journey that radically changed his approach to ministry. He began to open his ears to hear

God's voice. As he began to spend significant amounts of time in prayer, he began to sense vision from the Lord for the church in Presque Isle. The Lord also helped him communicate that vision more effectively.

As Rick led this journey for himself and the congregation, incredible things began to happen. One day as he was walking along a trail and praying, he sensed the Lord telling him thirty people were going to be saved at an upcoming youth event. He realized God was prompting him to share this at the next service *prior* to the youth event.

Rick says, "I questioned that. I didn't want to take that risk. However, I was convicted by God and knew that I was supposed to do that." The largest crowd they had ever had at any youth event was around 200 people. This event was attended by 470 people, and there was not enough room to hold them all. They decided to just cram the people in. At the end an invitation was given, and people were asked to stand up in their seats indicating a decision to receive Christ (since there was no room to move around due to the crowd). Exactly thirty people made that commitment.

On another occasion pastor Rick told me that as he was praying he sensed the Lord directing him to take a prayer team to a mountain in the area and pray that God would send people from the north, south, east and west to the church. The next week fifty new people visited the church. Today the church is averaging around 725 in weekend services.

As Rick described these events to me, I asked, "Every church would say they believe in prayer. What is different about how your church believes in prayer?"

He responded, "Prayer is not something we do. It is who we are . . . Prayer is not one of the anchor stores in the mall of Presque Isle Wesleyan Church, it is the entire foundation. Everything else is built on that."

I then asked how they made this kind of prayer practical and lived it out day in and day out. Here are some of the ways they integrate prayer into their daily lives:

- They do a weekly prayer service called "Highest Priority," based on the model from Brooklyn Tabernacle. Current average attendance is 125 adults, and 75 children and students.

- There is an active men's prayer team that supports the pastor.

- When they hold a congregational business meeting to vote on officers for the coming year, they meet, distribute the ballots, then ask people to go somewhere to pray for the Lord's direction. Only after this individual time of prayer do they gather collectively to pray and finally cast their ballots.

- They put a cross in their worship center and have concrete nails driven in the cross to represent people they are praying for who are without Christ. When a person gets saved, they tie a red ribbon around that nail. There are now 1000 nails and 207 with red ribbons around them. This represents not only a commitment to pray, but to share the gospel with the person, thus linking prayer with evangelism.

- There is a yearly prayer summit where they meet with key lay leaders and pastoral staff and spend from 9 a.m. to 9 p.m. in prayer for four straight days.

- Once each month they hold a men's prayer summit.

- There are men's and women's prayer teams.

- There are approximately 200 men who have committed to pray daily for their wives. (They call this the Ebenezer Project.)

- The staff meets for a thirty-minute prayer meeting *every morning*.

They have put feet to this idea that prayer is not what they do but is who they are. Pastor Rick said, "We have just tried to pursue God, and growth has been the by-product. We have never had numerical goals."

This is a church with a clear vision. Everything they do has prayer at its foundation. I asked Pastor Rick what would happen if I randomly asked fifty people from the church, "What is the main thing at Presque Isle Wesleyan Church?" He responded, "Every one of them would answer that prayer is the main thing at our church." That tells me the people of the congregation, the lay leadership, and the staff all have a clear picture of what their church is called to do and be.

I am not suggesting every church should have this same approach to ministry; however, I am contending that every church needs to have this kind of clarity about who they are and what they do. When that happens, God's Spirit is released in the lives of people who are given clear direction. The Scripture says, "If the trumpet does not sound a clear call, who will get ready for battle?" (1 Cor. 14:8). Praise the Lord for churches like Presque Isle Wesleyan Church who are sounding a clear call and are being used by God to enlarge the kingdom of God in a dark world.

PRAYER HITS HOME FOR PASTOR

Jim Cymbala, pastor of Brooklyn Tabernacle, tells a story in his book *Fresh Wind, Fresh Fire* that is an amazing example of God answering the prayers of His people. Jim and Carol Cymbala's daughter Chrissy had turned her back on God and had gone her own way, causing a great deal of heartache for them as parents. They had prayed deeply and often for their daughter to turn her heart back to God, but she determinedly went her own way. In the book, Jim Cymbala writes:

> February came. One cold Tuesday night during the prayer meeting, I talked from Acts 4 about the church boldly calling on God in the face of persecution. We entered into a time of prayer, everyone reaching out to the Lord simultaneously.
>
> An usher handed me a note. A young woman whom I felt to be spiritually sensitive had written: "Pastor Cymbala, I feel impressed that we should stop the meeting and all pray for your daughter."
>
> . . . .
>
> To describe what happened in the next few minutes, I can only employ a metaphor: The church turned into a labor room. The sounds of women giving birth are not pleasant, but the results are wonderful. Paul knew this when he wrote, "My dear children, for whom I am again in the pains of childbirth until Christ is formed in you" (Gal. 4:19).
>
> There arose a groaning, a sense of desperate determination, as if to say, "Satan, you will not have this girl. Take your

hands off her—she's coming back!" I was overwhelmed. The force of that vast throng calling on God almost literally knocked me over.[1]

When Pastor Cymbala returned home that evening, he explained what had happened and told his wife Carol that the battle for Chrissy was over. Just over a day later, as he was shaving, Carol burst into the room to tell him that Chrissy was home and was asking to see him. She begged their forgiveness and sought the forgiveness of God, then pointedly asked who it was that had prayed for her return. Chrissy said:

> "In the middle of the night, God woke me and showed me I was heading toward this abyss. There was no bottom to it—it scared me to death. I was so frightened. I realize how hard I've been, how wrong, how rebellious. But at the same time, it was like God wrapped his arms around me and held me tight. He kept me from sliding any farther as he said, 'I still love you.' "Daddy, tell me the truth—who was praying for me Tuesday night?"[2]

As I wrote at the beginning of this chapter, it is not enough for us to have churches and organizations that pray. We must build praying churches and praying organizations. This story of the Cymbala family and their church's powerful prayer ministry, is more telling than any words I could offer to illustrate what happens when we take the value of prayer to a whole new level—when we make deep and serious prayer part of the DNA of our churches and our personal lives.

SEEING THE FUTURE

1. Take few minutes to pray, asking God to speak to you about what you have just read in this chapter. Are there things He wants to speak to you about, things He wants to "burn into your heart," things He wants you to act upon?

2. Describe the "prayer temperature" of your church or organization.

3. Describe your personal prayer life.

4. How might you increase the effectiveness of your own prayer life? How might you make prayer a more integral part of your church or organization?

CHAPTER SIX

ENABLING VISION BY RECRUITING STAFF

—ɯᴗ—

> *People underestimate their capacity for change. There is never a right time to do a difficult thing. A leader's job is to help people have vision of their potential.*
> —Anonymous

I t was 1996, and Brendon Jones had just graduated from college with a degree in pastoral ministry. He interviewed with several churches but finally accepted a position at Meadville Community Church as minister of music and youth. At the time the church was averaging 350 on Sunday mornings and was showing a four-year pattern of growth with no indications that pattern would change in the near future. The senior pastor was an excellent teacher, a gifted worship leader, and a good organizational leader. Brendon was the second assistant pastor the senior pastor had hired. The other assistant pastor, Chuck Berg, was serving in the area of senior adult and single's ministry. There was a weekly staff meeting that all three pastors regularly attended.

As the church continued to grow, the demands of ministry grew. Growth necessitated that they add a second morning worship service and initiate a building program. The senior pastor discovered the need for more policies and procedures to help manage the larger number of people. There was a growing need for a part-time person to handle business affairs. The volunteer treasurer was overwhelmed with payroll, accounts payable, financial reports, and planning for a new building project. The senior pastor found himself chairing the local board meetings, participating in the building and long-range planning committees, leading the sermon planning team, and preparing the worship music on a weekly basis. It was getting to be a heavy load.

Brendon was seeing great results in youth ministry. The group grew from fifty middle- and high-school students combined, to fifty middle-school students and fifty high-school students. At the same time, the music ministry he led also was expanding. The choir was growing and was planning their first major musical production. A new worship team and band was assisting the senior pastor in leading worship. He also started a youth worship band, a youth ensemble, and two drama teams—one for youth and one for adults. Brendon, too, was feeling overwhelmed.

While all of this was going on, Chuck was seeing growth in both the single's ministry and in the ministry to senior adults. He started an outreach for divorce recovery and was flooded with community response because no other church in town offered this ministry. The senior adults began to plan outreach activities to share the gospel of Jesus Christ with other senior adults. This caused their group to grow as well.

Every week at least one person made the decision to become a Christ follower. That necessitated the need for follow up, which also necessitated the need for someone to train the lay people of the church to disciple those new believers. Someone had to step in and help them get connected in the church. Someone needed to help them find a place of belonging and a place of ministry. Someone needed to care for the children who seemed to multiply every week. Who would run the nursery? Who would lead the small groups? Who would equip new small group leaders? Who would teach the Sunday school classes? Who would help lead the youth group, which was going to need to split into two groups: middle school and high school?

About this time the senior pastor asked each of the staff members to take on new responsibilities to help manage the growth. The staff members saw the need and gladly stepped in to help.

Brendon agreed to take on music, youth (middle school and high school), children's ministry, and small-group leader training. Chuck took on single adults, senior adults, adult Sunday school, the welcome class for new families, and training of lay people for new-Christian follow up. The senior pastor added baptism orientation, new members class, and leadership training to his portfolio and began teaching a Sunday school class between services.

The church continued to grow, and the job descriptions continued to grow. The church added pastoral staff and support staff, which allowed an ongoing ebb and flow of everyone's job description. The staff of this church often consoled each other by saying, "I know a lot of churches that would love to have these problems."

So what's the problem? Leaders in these kinds of churches find themselves doing things out of necessity rather than out of passion or gifting. Because they are generally people who want to serve and build the Kingdom they are "get it done" kind of people. But when we decide to become a church that is focused, a church with a clear vision, it is important that we have staff, both paid and volunteer, functioning in the areas of their gifts and passions as much as possible.

With that in mind, in this chapter we'll discuss the issues of finding and equipping the right volunteer teams; in the next chapter we will address leading the full-time staff and leadership team. This will undoubtedly mean transition and change for some staff members, but it will be worthwhile.

FINDING THE RIGHT PERSON

When I was visiting Willow Creek Community Church I had an opportunity to meet with Joe Horness, one of the worship leaders at the church. Joe explained that Willow Creek had undertaken a major initiative to help people identify their spiritual gifts and use them in Kingdom service. He explained that at Willow Creek much of the facility cleaning is done by volunteers. All of the vacuum cleaners are repaired and maintained by volunteers. Hundreds of volunteers staff all the conferences the church hosts. Volunteers also serve outside the church in extension ministries to the poor and marginalized people of the Chicago area.

As Joe was describing the impact of those servants on the church, I began to imagine how all of these people, using their gifts in service to their local church, must have positively impacted their budget. I mentioned that observation to Joe.

He responded, "Yes, there is a positive impact on the church budget, but that is minor in comparison to the joy we have seen flood people's faces as they have discovered the gifts God has given them and have experienced the fulfillment of being in the trenches of ministry. We have seen people come alive in new ways."

I was convicted that my view was so narrow in thinking only of the budget. Joe helped raise my sights to the greater calling of helping people discover, develop, and deploy the spiritual gifts and passions God has given them.

Thinking about the example of that volunteering body of believers, I became convicted of something else I've been guilty of more times than I'd like to admit. If you ever are in need of volunteers in your work or ministry, perhaps you can relate. I pick up the phone, call John Doe and ask if he would be willing to help us out at the church by teaching fourth grade boys next year. After he recovers from the shock, he says, "I suppose I could help out for a while if no one else is willing to do it." I thank him, hang up the phone, and think, *Whew! I've got that one covered.*

There may not be anything wrong with the request, or even the answer, but I've too often forgotten a crucial preliminary step: I have taken little or no time to pray and ask God to guide me to someone He has in mind to teach that class. I have not taken into consideration the gifts God has given or not given to John Doe. I have demonstrated little concern about whether or not John Doe has any passion or interest in this ministry. My agenda was to get the base covered.

So often we can be guilty of using people and loving our agendas. The example of Willow Creek reminds us that we must be about the business of loving people and guiding them into areas of ministry that use the gifts and passions God has given them and that bear the kind of fruit God desires.

When we take time to do that, everyone wins. If this is where God has called John Doe to serve, he will teach his heart out. The fourth grade boys will think he is the greatest. He will serve when he's tired. He will serve when it's tough. He will serve when the boys give him a hard time. He will do all of this because he's serving God rather than a person's agenda. A call and affirmation from God will carry him in the great times and in the impossible times. Alternately, though, if he is only serving because I twisted his arm, he will burn out and be gone in a short time.

IDENTIFYING GIFTS

Having a clear and focused vision makes it more attractive for people to deploy their spiritual gifts into ministries that are the best fit. In many of our churches, we simply take the next willing person without regard for his or her spiritual wiring. This often results in burned out, tired, drained volunteers. The effectiveness of our corporate ministry and the personal fulfillment of the individual will be greatly enhanced as we deploy people in their gift areas.

If we are going to fulfill the vision we believe the Lord has given us, it is crucial that we have people who have identified and developed their spiritual gifts. We cannot carry out a God-sized vision with people who are burned out and are just trying to help cover a base.

With that in mind, if your church is going to make significant strides in fulfilling God's vision for you, you will need to help people identify the gifts God has entrusted to them and help them find ways to employ those gifts in tangible, vision-targeted ministry.

S.H.A.P.E.

At Saddleback Community Church they use a curriculum they call S.H.A.P.E. to help people discover how and where God wants to place them into His service. The program identifies and measures five things.

1. Spiritual Gifts—this is in the form of a test that helps identify the spiritual gift or gifts God has given you. In this portion of the curriculum, each person answers a series of questions designed to help identify those specific areas where God has supernaturally gifted him or her. There are a number of spiritual gifts listed in Scripture (Rom. 12:6–8, 1 Cor. 12:1–11, Eph. 4:11–13).[1]

2. Heart—This helps identify areas of passion. It helps each participant articulate what it is that keeps him up at night thinking about how God could use him. What does he find himself writing on the back of a napkin while having lunch at a restaurant? What does he find himself talking about with others? These are the things that are close to his heart and the things about which he has great passion.

3. Abilities—This represents the natural abilities God has given from birth. This may have to do with organization, creativity, music, speaking, an ability to notice what needs to be done, leadership, etc. When we surrender these abilities to God He often takes our natural abilities and calls us to use them for His glory and for building His Kingdom. So, it is valuable to have a clear understanding of what those abilities are.

4. Personality—This is a test that measures and helps identify the personality type God has given each person. The program identifies and explains four basic personality profiles.

5. Experiences—Life experiences can have a tremendous effect on us. When we include them in our total picture, they help us see purpose for the things God has either brought or allowed into our lives. How many times have we seen a person who has lost a child become an incredible comfort to someone else who has lost a child? We have all seen God use someone who has been through a battle with cancer used by God to help another cancer sufferer. These are life experiences that God can use in powerful ways.[2]

When you put all five of those areas together, you begin to see a picture of some ways God may want to use each person in ministry. When S.H.A.P.E. is used at its best, it also includes a personal consultation with a trained consultant to help the person find how his or her S.H.A.P.E. lines up with opportunities the church or community may have available.

I recently talked with a man at church who described what it has been like for him to discover a way to use his S.H.A.P.E. Our church has a large group of volunteers who help mow the twenty-five-acre lawn. When he found that he could ride a mower, be helpful to the church, and not have be in front of people to be serving Christ, he signed up right away. He has thoroughly enjoyed serving the Lord through this practical ministry in a way that fits his S.H.A.P.E.

Instead of going through the comprehensive S.H.A.P.E. curriculum, you might use one of the spiritual gifts tests mentioned in Appendix B.

RECRUIT! RETAIN! REWARD!

Identifying gifts is a start. But it is just part of the process. The issue that follows naturally is using what you've learned to train and place people in ministries that maximize their gifts.

Southeast Christian Church (SECC) in Louisville, Kentucky, has adopted a strategy that they have given the moniker: "Volunteers: Recruit! Retain! Reward!" The church developed a full program that not only helps people identify their gifts, but recruits people to use their gifts in service in the local church and community. The program provides tangible opportunities for people to test their gifts by trying a variety of ministries rather than simply continuing to do things they have been doing out of pure duty. In this way, they discover what gifts they have and how God wants to use those gifts. The program also requires all staff members to list volunteer development as one of their top five goals.

SECC also has developed means to help retain people in ministries where they are serving. This includes such practical things as an ongoing training program. The program is designed to minimize the risk of placing inadequately trained or unmentored people in places of service.

Additionally, as part of the reward for volunteers, SECC leadership works to show appreciation and give recognition along the way. This includes tangible recognition like notes of appreciation, public recognition, small gifts, and phone calls from a supervisor.

Willow Creek, too, has established a tradition of recognizing volunteers. Each year they ask all volunteers to come to the stage. Then they ask the congregation to say loudly, "We hold you in high regard. Way to go!" The audience cheers with great energy and enthusiasm. I have been there when they have done that, and it is a moving time. Even at the leadership conferences they host, Willow Creek's pastors look for ways to express appreciation and give public recognition to all the volunteers who serve. They rightly recognize the importance of affirming and encouraging those who take the gifts God has given them and place those gifts into service. This recognition motivates them to continue developing and using those gifts.

DEVELOPING VOLUNTEERS

If you are interested in taking this ministry to the next level in your church, my recommendation would be to begin (in light of what we discussed in chapter 5) by forming a prayer team around the specific issue of developing volunteers to serve the Lord through the ministry of your church.

After (and during) prayer, you'll want to identify key people who are gifted and would be willing to be trained on how to administer the spiritual gift inventory you choose. (We've already mentioned the S.H.A.P.E. material. You also could use Network from Willow Creek Community Church. Or you might check with other churches in your area to see what material has worked for them. Perhaps you could train your people alongside theirs. See Appendix B for more suggestions.)

Next, create a list of the ministries of your church and the preferred spiritual gifts that would best serve in that ministry. You can do this manually or with a database. You can then use that to help match people up with areas where their profile indicates a good fit. The personal consultation following the spiritual gift inventory will be a great help with this matching.

PLACING VOLUNTEERS

Once you have a trained team in place, you'll be able to offer a weekend seminar for the people of your church to come and take the S.H.A.P.E. class or another spiritual gifts inventory you choose. Make sure the times of the seminar are set with the convenience of the participants in mind.

On the Sunday following the seminar, offer a ministry fair for your congregation. Ask all of the ministries to set up displays that represent what their ministry does and what kinds of volunteers they need. Include in the worship service a couple of testimonies of people who are currently serving in each area. Look for those who find service particularly fulfilling and meaningful. Make sure the person is prepared and that you have reviewed their testimony with them beforehand so you put the person in a winning situation. Others will be drawn to this ministry just because of this person's contagious passion and enthusiastic spirit.

Follow up immediately on all the people who express interest. The more quickly you can expose them to the ministry, the greater opportunity to get them into a place of service. But be sure to plan ahead. Don't ask people to serve immediately. Create enough time so they can pray and seek the mind of the Lord about this ministry opportunity.

Another idea would be to create opportunities where people can try a variety of ministries before they commit to serve in a specific ministry. You might invite people to attend a children's class, a choir rehearsal, or a small group just to see how that ministry works. This will give them initial exposure without a commitment to get involved. Once they experience this ministry, they are more able to discern whether God is calling them to that area of service.

INVEST IN VOLUNTEERS

Make sure you train, motivate, and develop the people who serve. Provide practical tools of training that will help them be more effective in their areas of service. For example, you might consider having a concierge from an area hotel train your ushers on what it means to have excellent "customer service." Or your might invite someone who is a gifted storyteller to meet with your children's workers to teach them how to effectively tell a story. Someone who is gifted in the use of computers could show teachers how they could use PowerPoint or other electronic media in the presentation of their lessons.

Another productive way to invest in volunteers is to give them practical training on the development of their own spiritual lives. Offer a personal prayer seminar. Equip them with tools about how to study the Bible. Teach them how to lead someone to faith in Christ. Discuss how to make a guest feel welcome. The list could go on and on.

Kay is a person in our church who came to observe in children's ministry and thought she could never serve in an up front capacity. She decided to come as a helper and work under another leader, Tracy, who was gifted with children. One week Tracy asked Kay to take the lead, and Kay almost got physically sick. She said she was scared to death and didn't know how she would make it through. When she was finished with the morning, though, she felt a great sense of fulfillment and joy. Not long afterward, Tracy and her husband were transferred to another state, and Kay took over leading that ministry. She served there for a number of years and described it as a great joy of her life. She even got her husband involved in serving with her, and it became a great joy for him as well. She is now on our paid staff in children's ministry — all because Tracy saw a gift in Kay that Kay didn't see in herself, and challenged her to step out of her comfort zone to use that gift.

This story also illustrates another valuable piece of volunteer development. There is great value in having experienced, fulfilled leaders and workers mentor and develop others. Kay was mentored by Tracy — a great joy for both women.

By applying this bit of knowledge to your own situation, you could identify key leaders who are gifted, fulfilled, and experienced and ask them to mentor and develop other people over the next year. Finding right matches and partners for the mentoring relationship is critical to the success of a mentoring ministry. Whole books are written about this process. If your ministry vision includes pursuing a formal mentoring program, you'll want to research and train in that process as well.

But let me offer this reminder: Once people are on the team, mentored, trained, and serving regularly, don't forget about them. Instead, affirm and encourage at every step just like the folks at Willow Creek and SECC do. Perhaps there are some people in your church who work in the human resource field. These individuals are usually gifted at finding ways to recognize and reward service. Ask them to get together and create a plan for recognizing and honoring those who serve in volunteer roles in your church. You'll be amazed at how using their gifts in this way will enhance the experience for all those who serve in the church.

SPREADING THE WORK

There is one more value of recruiting and training gifted volunteers that we haven't mentioned—it allows for ownership and association with the ministry for the widest breadth of individuals. Who among us hasn't observed a church or ministry setting where one person is doing more than 50 percent of the work? This will always be an unhealthy situation—because not only will that person burn out eventually, but others will not be challenged to catch the vision and apply their own creativity to enhance the whole in ways one person simply couldn't accomplish.

If we are going to be successful at helping our churches focus on specific ministry with a clear vision, it is of utmost importance that we help the greatest number of individual people to focus on using the specific gifts God has given them to work toward achieving the common vision.

SEEING THE FUTURE

1. Take few minutes to pray, asking God to speak to you about what you have just read in this chapter. Are there things He wants to speak to you about, things He wants to "burn into your heart," things He wants you to act upon?

2. To what degree are you just "covering the bases" when filling positions rather than recruiting people based on their gifts and passions?

3. List the last five things you have done to train the volunteers with whom you work. How satisfied are you with those efforts? If there are volunteers who need additional training, what will you do to provide it within the next thirty days?

4. Do you have a process in place to help people discover, develop, and deploy their spiritual gifts? If not, what steps will you take to implement such a process?

5. In what ways do you reward those who serve in your organization? How might you improve on your efforts in this area?

CHAPTER SEVEN

ENABLING VISION BY EMPOWERING LEADERS

—ᴍᴍ—

> *Leadership is the art of getting someone else to do*
> *something you want done because he wants to do it.*
> —Dwight Eisenhower

A number of years ago I sat in my senior pastor's office as we shared with a staff member that he was going to need to find another place of ministry. I was shocked to hear him respond, "You don't know how freeing that is to me. I have known I was not wired for this ministry but didn't know how to gracefully get out of it." Now, everyone does not respond that way. However, that person left the staff and went on to a ministry that was fulfilling and meaningful for him and fruitful for the body of Christ.

This example illustrates the next focus of our clear vision quest: namely, that the right staff members need to be positioned in the right leadership roles for the vision to become a reality. Bill Hybels, senior pastor of Willow Creek Community Church often says, "How great it is to have churches that are led by people with the gift of leadership, taught by the people with the gift of teaching, administrated by those with the gift of administration, and served by those with the gift of serving." This statement could be continued to include all of the spiritual gifts.

Jim Collins, in his book *Good to Great,* uses the metaphor of a bus to describe the secret to staffing an organization successfully. He says:

> The executives who ignited the transformations from good to great did not first figure out where to drive the bus and then get people to take it there. No, they first got the right people on the bus (and the wrong people off the bus) and then figured out where to drive it. If we get the right people on the bus, the right people in the right seats, and the wrong people off the bus, then we'll figure out how to take it someplace great.[1]

For this scenario to move from theory to reality, staff may need to go through the same process of identifying gifts as we discussed in the previous chapter when we talked about volunteers.

GETTING THE RIGHT PEOPLE ON THE BUS

Think back to the example of the growing church you read about at the beginning of chapter six. Remember how the staff positions were undergoing an ebb and flow to allow all the bases to be covered? And consider how stretched—and probably stressed—the associate pastors and staff members must have felt as their primary ministry visions had to be diluted to make room for the addition of responsibilities that may just have been outside their callings and giftings.

The leadership of your church may need to engage in a process to help identify the gifts, passions, and desires of each member of the staff. This will also need to include a process for some staff to transition from present roles to new roles and may require major change for the staff and for the church.

There will be three possible results that will come from this process: One, the staff member will discover and affirm that he or she is in the right role, employing the gifts, passions, and desires that God has given. Praise the Lord, and celebrate that. Two, the staff member will discover that his or her gifts are in line with where the church is going but he or she will need to make a change in current roles. This will involve a process of communication and adjustment for other staff, lay leaders, and the staff member. Third, the staff member will either self discover or have someone else help him or her discover that the gifts, passions, and desires he or she has don't fit into the future of that ministry. This is the most difficult scenario—for the person, the other staff, and the church. This does not mean the person is not gifted, is not liked, and is not good at what he or she does. It simply means that the person will need to find that place in the Kingdom where his or her God-given gifts can be fully used.

A WORKABLE PROCESS

Let me share one possible way to do this process of evaluation. I am indebted to Don Cousins for some of the ideas expressed here.

1. Ask each staff member to take one of the spiritual gifts tests described in chapter six.

2. Next, ask each staff member to take the Personality Dynamic Profile (PDP) test or another appropriate personality inventory. This test will need to be professionally scored and interpreted but will be well worth the effort.[2]

3. Then take a pad of paper and a pen and go to a quiet spot where you can pray and listen to the Lord. As you pray, ask the Lord to speak to you and affirm those things He has called you to be and do. As those things come to mind write them down. Next, make a list of things you think about when you have time to reflect about your life and ministry. What are the things that keep you up at night thinking and praying? What are the things you jot notes about on napkins at a restaurant? What are the things you've always dreamed of doing? Finally, answer the question, "What would I do if I knew I couldn't fail?" The Passion and Heart Exercise mentioned in Appendix B might assist you with this process also.

4. Your next step is to compile the results from all of the previous materials to begin to create a profile of how the person's gifts, personality, strengths, weaknesses, and passions fit with what he is being asked to do in his present job description. You may experience great benefit from having a person outside the church assist with the process of evaluating all of this material. Who among us can be objective and unbiased about

ministries, programs, and people when we have a personal stake in their future? This is also an area that requires great prayer and great care. It is not something to rush or force.

5. Finally, in collaboration with the staff member and the leadership of the church, make appropriate decisions about what the results of this process tell you.

INVEST IN STAFF AND LEADERSHIP

Once all the right people are on the bus and in the right seats, you'll want to turn your attention to training and development. Investing in the ongoing training and development of the members of staff and lay leadership—beginning with senior staff—will pay big dividends. You'll want to help all participants see training and development not as a cost but as an investment, a significant ongoing need, and a priority to most effectively accomplish the organization's vision. You'll find it most important to cast this vision with those who control budgets. Many times their unwillingness to fund such items is because they don't understand the impact these expenditures can have on the life of the church. Thriving churches consider staff development a high priority and are using a number of creative methods to accomplish it.

The following scenario illustrates the importance of staff development. Consider sharing this story with those who work on the budget for your church or organization.

I remember the first hospital visit I did as a pastor. The church I was serving was led by a senior pastor who was a wonderful person but did not understand or appreciate the value of training and equipping the staff. He assumed we knew what we were doing, so when he was preparing to leave on vacation, he called me into his office and asked me to visit Mrs. Johnson while he was gone. That was the extent of the training. I did not go to seminary and had not planned to go into the ministry when I was in college, so I did not have any formal ministry training or experience. I did not know that Mrs. Johnson was unconscious. I did not know Mr. Johnson did not profess to know the Lord. I did not know that most of the family members were nominally connected to the church. I did not know Mrs. Johnson was dying from cancer. I had no idea what to do when I went to the hospital. So I floundered. And to this day I remember with sorrow the lost opportunity to share Christ's comfort skillfully and compassionately with this grieving family, at a time when it could have made a real difference in their eternal destiny.

I compare that instance to hospital visits I make today, now that I have both experience and training to help equip me for the task. Now I am conscious of ways to help the family sense the presence of the Lord, ways to encourage and help them through this difficult time.

Which pastor would you rather have visit with you and your family in such a time? One who is uncomfortable and ill equipped, or one who is trained and ready to offer prayer and real comfort?

PROFESSIONAL AND TEAM DEVELOPMENT

Now that you understand the value of team training and development, let's turn our attention toward ways to accomplish it in the lives of each staff member. Again, we'll go to school on the examples of some of the churches I studied in my research.

MISSION STATEMENTS

Centenary United Methodist Church requires all staff members to begin writing a life mission statement within six months of employment. After one year they are required to write a ministry vision statement. Those statements are used as a guide in the staff development and training process. The goal is to see each staff person working in his or her area of calling, giftedness, and passion. This is a way to invest in staff and make a statement to the staff members that they are valued. It is also a way to express a desire to see them become more effective and productive.

CONFERENCES AND SPECIAL EVENTS

In many churches, ministry staff members attend conferences and ministry-specific training events together for professional development and team building, funded by the church.

Most of the churches I visited have regularly scheduled in-house training meetings. Some take advantage of local resources by inviting teachers and leaders who visit their area to address the staff. For example, Brentwood Baptist Church is located near Nashville, home to a number of Christian publishing houses. Brentwood frequently contacts those publishers to invite visiting authors to remain in the area for an extra day and meet with church staff.

In your church, events might center around a book that all staff members have studied, a video series, a presentation by a staff member, or a team-building activity that includes an element of good, old-fashioned fun.

Alternately, churches of similar philosophy and size often partner for staff development. Staff counterparts may meet periodically, with occasional gatherings of their entire combined staffs.

PROFESSIONAL CONSULTATIONS

Some organizations have made financial investments to hire professional consultants, job coaches, or training firms. Kingdom Building Ministries, for example, has made use of such services, and the strategy has proven to be fruitful and cost effective. They intentionally maintain a lean staff, and they believe the occasional hiring of consultants has allowed them to gain needed professional acuity and specialized expertise without having to expend resources to hire additional staff for the long term. Historically, they have seen outside consultants provide outstanding stewardship of both human and financial resources.

MENTORS

Some churches form small leadership huddles where an experienced staff member (perhaps the senior pastor) meets with a group of younger staff to study a book, review teaching video tapes, and discuss how these may apply to the ministry. These mentoring relationships have great value through investing in the people who are currently leading and who will lead in the future.

AREAS TO TARGET

While much of the training and development you undertake will be specifically related to the giftings and ministries of individual team members, there are some areas of common need for training that could serve the added benefit of helping in the area of team building and camaraderie. I've purposely included a long list here, so there are many options for you to choose from and many ways to address these areas in ongoing team training. Thinking long-term, if you decide to offer a special staff training once a month or even just four times per year, you'll need lots of fresh ideas and topics to keep excitement and energies high. So pick and choose from the following partial list, and then come up with areas of your own where you think your overall team could most benefit from group training.

COMMUNICATIONS

This could include areas such as how to develop a promotional ad, how to write an article for the newsletter, how to write a report or a proposal for the board to consider, how to use PowerPoint or other presentation software. It could also include learning to ask the right questions, such as, Who gets affected by this decision? Who should we tell about this change? Should this be done in writing, in person, by e-mail, etc.? What is my body language saying? What forms of communication are available to me?

There are people in your local schools, area churches, or other organizations who are gifted speakers who could come to meet with you and share techniques of preparation and delivery for public speaking. There are also training events such as Carol Kent's Speak Up With Confidence seminars and Florence and Marita Littauer's Christian Leaders and Speakers Services (CLASS) that are available for developing this area of ministry.

Another area of communications that is key, but might be overlooked, is the area of sermon preparation. One suggestion would be to ask a few pastors in your area from your denomination or from other churches to meet for an extended lunch and share how they go about the process of sermon preparation. You will be amazed at the insights that will come from just asking others to describe what they are doing. Everyone at the luncheon will probably walk out with at least one useable new idea.

CONFLICT RESOLUTION

We all face conflict at some time or another. How do we respond to it effectively? Teaching people to use "I" statements rather than "you" statements is helpful. Distinguishing between assertive, passive, aggressive, and passive-aggressive behavior is helpful. These are valuable insights in resolving conflict. You could hold a training session that seeks to answer the questions: What's the difference between personal conflict and professional conflict? And how do we handle conflict within a committee or board?

TIME AND CALENDAR MANAGEMENT

There are many resources available to do training on time management. Perhaps some of the business people in your congregation have been through some training that they could present to you, your volunteer leaders and your staff. We invited a person from a local business who was part of our congregation to train us on the use of GroupWise, which is an e-mail, calendar, task list management tool on our computers. It proved to be helpful to us and was fulfilling for the parishioner as well.

LEADERSHIP DEVELOPMENT

There are books, video series, tape series, and printed materials that deal effectively with leadership development and training. I subscribe to e-mail groups that provide regular articles dealing with leadership development. I read books from the church environment as well from the business environment that are helpful in growing as a leader.

The Leadership Summit at Willow Creek Community Church is one of many conferences that focus on this area of need. Southeast Christian Church in Louisville, Kentucky, also sponsors an annual leadership conference. If possible, it is great to go to one of these conferences as a group, stay overnight, and debrief at the end of each day. I have had valuable and meaningful conversations with fellow staffers that have helped put the lessons of that day's conference into clearer perspective.

A subcategory in leadership development would be an issue we addressed very early in this book, namely managing change. We never can get enough training on how to manage change. There are books you can purchase and study as an individual or as a group. Inviting people from other churches, organizations, or businesses who have successfully been through significant change to come and speak is another way to get training and insight into this important issue that faces all of us every day.

TEAM BUILDING

Do a team-building exercise on building teams. Presumably each member of your leadership team is responsible for leading at least one team of people, but not everyone has the right training for team leadership. A team-building exercise will teach your leaders to do things together, plan together, pray together, read and study together, brainstorm together, and serve together. Because one idea that helps build a sense of team with any group is to take a personality profile together and learn how each person is wired by God, you might do a training event on how to administer and interpret one of these profiles. It will help everyone on the team be more understanding of the way others process things, come alongside others in areas of their weakness, and allow others to come alongside them in their own areas of weakness.

CONDUCTING A HOSPITAL VISIT

In light of the story I told earlier in this chapter, perhaps asking someone who has been in the hospital and has experienced a meaningful visit to come and tell her story would be beneficial for the entire team. Another way to accomplish this training would be to ask a seasoned pastor to share how he conducts a hospital visit. Some local hospitals have chaplains who would be willing to come and do training for you, your lay volunteers, and your staff.

TOOLS FOR EFFECTIVE COUNSELING

Let me caution you to not try and turn every leader into a professional psychologist. However, there are some basic techniques you can learn about how to help people with a variety of issues in their lives. Developing good listening skills can be a great asset. Learning how to help people make effective decisions and how to communicate more effectively can make a difference. Perhaps a local Christian counselor would be willing to do basic training on how to recognize when to refer someone to a professional.

COMPUTERS AND TECHNOLOGY IN MINISTRY

There are incredible things available in audio, video, lighting, digital technology, and computers that have applications in ministry. Organizations like Focus on the Family are regularly using digital technology, satellite technology, desktop publishing, and many other modern tools to enhance their ministries.

We have done a number of training sessions showing people how they can use the computer for valuable ministry resources. We can use computers to organize music libraries, sermon notes, meeting minutes, manage ministry budgets, and design graphically attractive flyers and promotional pieces. We can use a computer for group communication, networking with people around the world, sharing the plan of salvation, and even praying for people. There are people in your church and community who would see it as a privilege to help you get more effective ministry use out of your computer. Don't be afraid to ask for their time.

Web site development, for example, can enable you to offer recordings of your pastor's sermons online at no charge to the end user. You can put a daily devotional on your church's Web site. You can create areas on a Web site where you can have confidential communication with board members. We use our Web site to post volunteer schedules for our technical ministry. Once we have trained our staff members well, their imaginations and our budgets will be about the only limitations in the area of technology.

On the flip side of this issue, we invited the local chief of police to come and share with one of our large Sunday school classes how computers are used in inappropriate ways in our community. There are undoubtedly people in your congregation who have been trained in how to help you guard against pornography and other inappropriate uses of computers. As a side note on this topic, we have installed software on all our computers to screen out inappropriate Web sites and have the ability to monitor what staff members are looking at on their computers. This ability has resulted in difficult conversations with folks who have violated some of the principles we hold deeply.

RECRUITING AND TRAINING VOLUNTEERS

One of the staff members at our church, Gayle Deur, is the most gifted recruiters of volunteers I have ever met. I have learned much from her just by asking questions and by observing how she approaches this task. There are people in your church or local non-profit community who are similarly gifted. Ask them if they would come to train you and your team.

Welcoming and Following Up

You might ask a customer service professional to meet with your ushers, greeters, and welcome center staff to suggest ways to make your church a more welcoming place.

Likewise, following up and connecting with people who have visited the church or who have made decisions to become Christ followers is crucial. But what are the best ways to accomplish those tasks? Staying in touch with what other churches are doing through ongoing training, visiting other churches, and reviewing other churches' printed materials are a few of the ways your team may grow together in this area.

Sharing Your Faith

Invite a new Christian to come and share with your volunteers, your board, and your staff. Seeing a real-live new Christian will motivate and inspire people. Use material put out by a variety of organizations to do formal training for evangelism. Find a person with the gift of evangelism and have them come and tell stories of how they have led someone to Christ. Consider inviting someone who is not a Christ follower to come and share his or her observations about his or her experiences.

Enhancing Personal Walks with Christ

There is no area of leadership development that will pay greater eternal dividends than helping your leadership team members deepen and broaden their personal relationships with Christ. One idea would be to study the Bible together by inviting an experienced person to lead you and your team through a process of studying a specific passage of Scripture. Another suggestion would be to set up accountability relationships for Scripture memorization.

If Scripture reading is key, so is deepening their prayer lives. As we mentioned earlier, creating meaningful opportunities for times of extended prayer is a terrific use of staff and team time. Share answers to prayer. Study key Bible passages on prayer together. Have a person who is a gifted intercessor share with your team.

Additionally, the list of books and resources on building the Christian life is endless. Learning to make the most of these resources is another good team exercise. Some people have systems they use when reading a book to help them get more out of it. These systems help them retain more of its information and help them retrieve that information easily. Look for someone with that gift and ask him or her to come in and share with your team. Another option would be to ask a variety of people how they read books and then report findings to your team.

TRAINING AND DEVELOPMENT TECHNIQUES

Once you have identified areas where you'd like to begin group training and development, how do you translate that vision into reality? Be creative here. But if you need something to jumpstart the process, try one of the following options:

1. Ask members of the staff to do training in an area where they are gifted.

2. Ask members of the congregation to do training in an area where they have vocational experience.

3. Make use of video training tools from a public, school, or college library.

4. Invite other pastors or staff member from other churches to come to your church and do training in an area of their expertise.

5. Identify a book your staff could study together. Create an environment that encourages full group participation.

6. Go to the Barna Web site, www.barna.org, read an article, and discuss its implications with your staff.

7. Do a phone interview with another pastor or leader. Prepare for this by preparing questions and setting a phone appointment with the person.

8. Invite a business person from your congregation to share with the staff a business principle that has applications for your ministry.

9. Ask members of your staff to meet for the purpose of sharing resources and ideas about a subject. You may be surprised at the resourcefulness of people who are around you every day.

10. Do a series of training and development sessions on the spiritual disciplines as practiced by some of the heroes of the faith by asking staff members to do a study on Bible heroes or historic Christians.

This area of staff transition and training is of critical importance if the members of your team are going to know what the vision of the church is and if they are going to know how to carry it out on a day-to-day basis.

Let's take a moment to revisit Meadville Community Church, which we introduced in chapter six. For the short term, the staff and lay leaders of the church stepped in to help do whatever they could to assist in leading this church through a time of significant growth. It was exciting; however, people could not continue long-term ministry in areas in which they were not gifted or passionate.

The senior pastor asked to meet with the board, key volunteer leaders, and staff in a combined meeting to begin addressing the long-term picture. Through a time of serious prayer, seeking God, sharing with one another, and formal evaluation, they were able to make some significant shifts in how they approached the future. Over a few months, they reorganized the board and placed people into areas of deep passion and gifting. Staff members' portfolios were shuffled and adjusted. Key lay leaders took on responsibilities in areas where they were passionate and gifted and were released to give strong leadership. The lights began to come back in people's eyes as they found themselves doing more of what they sensed God had placed them on earth to do.

They also discovered they could let go of many of the things they had been doing. Some of those ministries died a natural death. Some were picked up by people who felt great passion for them. Some were able to continue in a maintenance mode until someone sensed God calling them to lead in that area.

After this time of change and adjustment, the church began to take on new life again. People were being trained and equipped to do the work of the ministry, both in the church and outside the church. There was a sense of purposefulness to the ministry and less of a sense of just trying to keep up. Stories of people being released into ministry in their workplace, their neighborhoods, the community, and the church began to emerge as they discovered their passions, gifts, and callings from God. The focus of board meetings began to change as the board began to hone in on the specific mission to which God had called this church. Their ministry became more proactive and less reactive as they continued to zero in like a laser on their specific demographics, the needs of their community, and the gifts and callings of the people God had brought to this church. Board meetings no longer consisted only of evaluating the financial reports and building reports. They began to focus on mission accomplishment and narrowing the vision for greater effectiveness.

Prayer took on a new meaning as the church began to launch into areas that depended on God showing up. Prayer moved beyond requests for physical healing to include passionate concern for reaching lost people, as well as finding the right people to lead a variety of efforts to win them.

The focus of ministry moved from being consumer-based to being mission-based. The leadership team developed a resolve of steel that God had called them to passionately reach lost people; to compassionately minister to marginalized people in their community; and to effectively equip believers to discover, develop, and deploy their gifts and passions into personal and corporate ministry. As they continued down this road, they also discovered there was great risk involved. Some of the people who had been comfortable in the old way of approaching ministry were not pleased with being moved out of their comfort zone.

This is a typical response. So in the next chapter we'll turn our attention to the risks we take when narrowing our focus to meet our prayerfully established clear vision.

SEEING THE FUTURE

1. Take few minutes to pray, asking God to speak to you about what you have just read in this chapter. Are there things He wants to speak to you about, things He wants to "burn into your heart," things He wants you to act upon?

2. Do you have the "right people on the bus" in your church or organization? List those "right people." Are they in the "right seat"?

3. Is there anyone in your church or organization who needs to be moved to a different seat or removed? Consider gaining counsel on this issue from some trusted, unbiased colleagues. Walk carefully in this area.

4. In what ways could you more effectively invest in the development and growth of key leaders in your organization, both paid staff and volunteers?

CHAPTER EIGHT

ENABLING VISION BY TAKING RISKS

—ww—

> *Obstacles are those frightful things you see when*
> *you take your eyes off your goal.*
> —Henry Ford

A few months ago I sat down with a financial advisor who was helping me sort out the best ways to prepare for my future retirement. He asked a lot of questions about how much I was able to invest and how much I already had invested. Then he asked, "How would you describe your risk tolerance? Do you watch the market every day to see how your funds are doing? If the funds go down for a period of time does it make you nervous?" He was trying to measure my willingness to take risks and my comfort with risk-taking.

Like every investor, churches also face decisions about risk. Because we may risk our reputation in the community or we may risk causing some people to feel isolated or hurt, we need to gauge our risk tolerance before embarking on a new venture. We must face the reality that some folks may choose not to embrace the change, may decide to withhold financial support, may move to another church, or may try to remove the leader who initiated the change.

COUNTING THE COST

As I visited a variety of ministries, I discovered that older, more established organizations find it harder to be innovative and creative. As they age, organizations become more conscious of image, more afraid to endure loss, and more cautious about how their reputations may be affected by change. They tend toward the we've-always-done-it-that-way response. One of the churches I visited acknowledged that they were on hold, waiting for the current senior pastor to retire. They did not want to rock the boat.

Younger, less established churches demonstrate a greater willingness to be different, try new things, and even fail. The clarity of their vision empowers them to tolerate the negative feedback that often arises from those who do not share their vision. I do not suggest that we should take wholesale risks just for fun. But I do believe that the willingness to venture increases creativity and creates an environment where staff and laity feel empowered to try new things even though they might fail or take some flak.

You must be willing to risk your reputation, your image, and your past success in order to thrive in the future. If you are not willing to increase your risk tolerance, it is possible that you will become "the church that used to be."

What are some of the risks we may encounter as we initiate prayerful change toward accomplishing our clear vision?

A CASE STUDY IN RISK ASSESSMENT

Adam and Christy Lipscomb wrestled in prayer during all of seminary, asking God to reveal a common vision for ministry for them when they graduated. It was a challenging, messy struggle. Eventually the couple was convinced that fresh out of seminary God was calling them to plant a church in the inner city of Grand Rapids.

The inner city of Grand Rapids has a significant amount of crime and is, as you might expect, an area that has many of the features of an urban area: drugs, prostitution, low-income housing, and other challenges. For many of us, that looks like a lot of risk for a young couple and a fledgling church plant to overcome. Yet when they sensed this was what God had called them to do, Adam and Christy were able to move ahead in the confidence that God would manage the risks they would face.

The couple categorizes the risks they are taking as different—but no greater—than the risks all of us should be taking when we abandon ourselves to following God's call on our lives. Adam and Christy challenge all of us—even those of us in established churches—to live in the center of God's design for our lives, which will involve risk whether we are church planting in an inner-city setting or serving in an established suburban church.

THE RISK OF BEING MISUNDERSTOOD

Our church in Holland learned a few lessons about risk tolerance when we began a serious outreach to divorcees. As we saw the issue at the beginning, we had to ask ourselves many risk tolerance questions: If we offer this ministry, will anyone come? What kind of a reputation will we develop in the community? Will people think we don't value marriage? Will people think we bless or condone divorce? Will this turn into a dating service for divorced people?

As we expected, some people did accuse us of not valuing marriage. Others said we condoned divorce and offered people a cheap way out.

Yet on the positive side, we have seen big dividends as a result of our investing in this risky business. Numbers of people have come to know Christ through this ministry, and through it God has brought healing to some broken marriages. We also launched a ministry called Restoring the Gift, that reaches out to couples who are in trouble but not yet divorced. This ministry, too, has born fruit of restoring broken and struggling marriages. All of these great results began with a willingness to take risks.

THE RISK OF LOSING NUMBERS

Although Kentwood Community Church in Grand Rapids, Michigan, took a risk in a different area, their experience was similar to ours in Holland. This church made a commitment to plant other churches in Greater Grand Rapids. One of the risks involved was that it meant people would leave Kentwood Community Church to attend the new church plant. Whenever the parent church is growing and increasing in number, they plant a church in a new area. Yes, numbers—both attendance and budgeted income—in the parent church go down when a new congregation is planted. But Kentwood's leadership team has chosen to have a Kingdom view rather than a personal empire view.

THE RISK OF SHAKING THINGS UP

One of the churches I visited sensed the Lord calling them to address issues of complacency, style of worship, facilities, leadership, and a variety of challenging concerns. As a result of making major changes that they believed were going to help them live out the vision to which the Lord had called them, many people complained and resisted. These were people who had gotten comfortable in the old way of doing church and did not want to change. It was a hard time for them and for the leadership, and within three years several hundred people decided to worship elsewhere. At the same time, though, several hundred new people came. Many of these were new believers who would never have been reached had the church not taken these courageous steps of faith. It was not an easy journey. It was anguishing at times. Yet it resulted in greater fruit for the Kingdom.

LEARNING FROM THE PAST

To manage risk taking effectively we must learn to balance two opposing values: the knowledge gained by experience versus a preference for the future. The temptation for future-looking ministries is to throw out the past. But Bill Hybels, in *Courageous Leadership*, cautions us against that temptation:

> Often staff members come to my office to promote ministry plans they want me to support. Sometimes, to their great surprise, I cut them off mid-sentence. "I've heard enough," I say. "Count me out." Thinking I'm kidding, they continue trying to convince me. So I jump in again, "No. Not in my lifetime. It's just not going to happen."
>
> By then they realize I'm serious. If they ask, "Why?" I might say something like this: "We tried that same thing fifteen years ago. We thought we were smart, but we got whacked. We tried it again ten years ago, and we got whacked again. Three years ago we took another pass at it, and we really got whacked. So we have far exceeded our whack tolerance. I understand why your proposal sounds good to you; it sounded good to us too. But it isn't good. So I mean it when I say this idea is DOA—dead on arrival. It's not going to happen, so just let it go."[1]

Over the years you may have been whacked a few times, too. You may be a leader who has taken risks—for good reasons—and failed. Many leaders in this situation have what Hybels calls a pain file, memories of good plans gone wrong. The contents of that file help to evaluate new ideas. In this way, we can indeed look to our experiences to help us evaluate the risks of future endeavors.

PREFERENCE FOR THE FUTURE

On the other hand, though, we must be willing to launch new initiatives and to relinquish some of the things that helped us get where we are today. We must be willing to let go of the past if we are to move forward.

Let me caution, though, that letting go of the past does not include letting go of the essentials of our faith. There are some things we should never abandon. We should never let go of our commitment to Scripture, the person of Christ, and a few other fundamental beliefs. To do so would be spiritual compromise. We must, however, be willing to let go of programs and approaches to ministry that were effective in bringing us to this point if they will not be effective in fulfilling our vision for the future.

About each current program and ministry we must ask, "Is this the *best* way to build fully devoted followers of Jesus Christ at *this* time and in *this* place?" That may lead to the closure of some well-loved ministries that have been effective until now. But it will undoubtedly be necessary if we are to fully empower new ministries that will propel us into the future.

Suppose you were in Los Angeles and wanted to go to New York City. While it would not be the fastest way to get there, a car would serve that purpose effectively. It would be a preferred mode of transportation if you also wanted to see and experience the country along the way. However, when you arrived in New York, if you decided you wanted to go to London, that car would no longer be effective as a mode of transportation. Even though it had served effectively to get you from where you had been to where you are, it would not work to get you to the next desired destination. Just like that car, there are times when trying to continue using methods and tools in ministry that have served us well along the road in the past will cause us to sink in the ocean of future work.

Balancing these two values—experience gained from the past and a preference for the future—is more art than science. There is no easy formula for decision making, yet it is critical if we are to increase our willingness to be significant risk takers for God.

IDENTIFYING AN ACCEPTABLE RISK

How do you know what an acceptable risk is? How do you go about evaluating your church's risk tolerance? At a recent Central Wesleyan Church staff retreat, there was a significant discussion about the current level of risk tolerance in our local church culture. This is a valuable and important discussion for every church to have. It is important to gain an understanding of the culture of risk at your church.

Risk taking is dangerous, of course, and some risks are simply not worth taking. As I did with my financial advisor, every organization should count these costs by evaluating and assessing risks before taking a plunge in a new direction. This analysis should be both ponderous and prayerful. This should never be done as a lone ranger. We should always involve other key leaders in this process. It is essential to spend time with staff, lay leadership, and the people of the congregation praying and seeking the mind of Christ when approaching significant change.

We might begin by asking—

- What are the risks involved in making this change?

- What are the people costs?

- What are the financial costs?

- What are the costs of *not* making this change?

- Who will be most affected?

- Who will be hurt the most?

- Who will be helped the most?

- How does this change affect our ability to live out our ministry vision?

- Is this change essential to achieving God's calling for our church?

AN HONEST ASSESSMENT

What are some of the specific risks that could be involved? These risks will include things like staff members or long-standing members of the church who may leave. There may be some favorite programs that need to come to a close. You may have to deal with a higher level of criticism for a period of time. There may need to be some significant revamping of children's ministry, student ministry, or public worship services. There may be changes in lay leadership needed to provide the expertise to lead into the future. You may need to reorganize administratively. That could result in some people feeling a loss of power. These are the normal risks that go with any change.

However, all of the costs are seldom easily identified. At Central Wesleyan we made a decision to start charging schools and other outside organizations when they wanted to use our facilities for community events. This helped us cover the costs of operation. It was easy to measure the cost to us when we did not charge those organizations to cover our operating costs. When we began to charge for the use of our facilities, those organizations found it more difficult to come and consequently chose to have their events at other places. What was more difficult for us to measure was the cost of not having those people and organizations come to our campus and experience the impact of being touched by our ministry. It was harder to measure the loss of good public relations in the community. It was difficult to measure how many families may have started attending our church because they were first exposed to it while attending their local high school graduation ceremony held in our worship center.

Just like the consideration of the cost of changing, we need to consider the obvious and hidden costs of *not* changing. Sometimes the price of *not* changing is greater than the price of changing. For example, it is easy to measure the cost of developing an Internet Web site for your church that is current, relevant, and user friendly. It is much more difficult to measure the cost of not doing that in today's technological, Internet savvy culture. It could be that the hidden cost of *not* offering a relevant Web site is much higher in the long run than the obvious cost of creating and maintaining one today.

It is important to find ways assess the risk, measure the cost, and evaluate what you sense the Lord is directing you to do. When you come to that place of peace, sensing that the Lord has given guidance, I urge you to press on and take the necessary risks.

MINIMIZING RISK

Note my last statement again. "Press on and take the *necessary* risks." Yes, there are some risks that just go with the territory. But there are other risks that can be controlled and minimized. So, as we move into the future, let's look at how we can minimize unnecessary risks.

First, spend significant amounts of time in prayer before jumping into a significant risk. Pray alone. Pray as a leadership team. Pray often until you have a deep sense of peace.

Next, determine whether you have a direction from Scripture about this risk. Is there anything about it that is not clearly supported by Scripture? Did God speak to you from His Word about moving in this direction? Are there principles from God's Word that speak to this issue?

Third, do your homework. Some people take risks just for the adrenaline rush and don't take time to prepare for the risks. I found it interesting to watch Robbie Knievel do a motorcycle jump on television a few months ago. I was amazed at all the preparation that had gone into that jump. There were teams of people evaluating the slope of the ramp, the wind conditions, and the mechanical condition of the motorcycle. They did their homework before taking such a major risk. They got all the right permits, measured the landing area, determined the G-forces, and much more. They did not go into this risk-taking adventure without a lot of hard preparatory work. And neither should we.

Finally, as you seek to minimize unnecessary risk, test your plans against the input of trusted, wise advisors. I would encourage you to surround yourself with some people who tend to be risk-takers and some people who tend to be more conservative. Listen to the feedback of both groups. Ask them what they sense God is telling them about taking this risk. Don't wait for a perfect consensus to move forward (you'll seldom achieve that), but don't discount the counsel from either group as you make your educated risk choices.

Above all, when considering moving into risky new waters, remember the counsel of Scripture. In 2 Timothy 1:7 Paul writes, "For God did not give us a spirit of timidity, but a spirit of power, of love and of self-discipline." Similarly, God told Joshua four different times to "be strong and courageous" as he led the Israelites (Josh. 1:6, 1:9, 1:18 and 10:25).

Life is filled with risks. We take a risk when we drive, when we fly, when we walk down the street. Let's not allow fear to impede our commitment to take great risks for the greatest cause of all, the kingdom of God.

SEEING THE FUTURE

1. Take few minutes to pray, asking God to speak to you about what you have just read in this chapter. Are there things He wants to speak to you about, things He wants to "burn into your heart," things He wants you to act upon?

2. What is the biggest personal risk you have taken in the last year? How would you describe your personal risk tolerance?

3. What is the biggest organizational risk you have taken in the last year? How would you describe your organization's risk tolerance? Would others agree with your assessment? Consider raising the issue for discussion with your colleagues.

4. What are some risks you believe need to be taken either by you personally or by your organization? What can you do to minimize the negative impact of those risks? What can you do maximize the positive impact of those risks?

CHAPTER NINE

ENABLING VISION BY MANAGING CHANGE

—ɯ—

> *Leadership is the capacity to translate vision into reality.*
> —Warren G. Bennis

I enjoy running. A few years ago I started having significant pain in my hips and knees as a result of running regularly. I mentioned this to a fellow staff member who suggested I go see Brad, a physical therapist who attends our church. I called Brad and asked if I could stop by and see him about some problems I was having as a runner. He invited me to his office for a visit the next morning.

In his office, we exchanged pleasantries. Then Brad asked me to describe the problem I was having and the routine I went through to run. I told him about pain in my left hip and left knee, both of which were severe after I finished running. I then shared my routine with him. I said, "I get dressed with a T-shirt, running shorts, and running shoes; go to my basement; turn on Super Nintendo Baseball; start my treadmill; and run between four and five miles at an 8.5 minute per mile pace while playing Super Nintendo Baseball. He looked at me, as if to ask, "Is that all?" When I didn't say anything else, he asked if I did any stretching or warming up. I told him I did a couple of knee bends and a back bend or two but other than that, nothing else.

For the next hour Brad taught me a series of pre-running warm-up stretches and exercises to use every time I run. He then talked about cooling down after I run. Once I began to practice those warm ups and cool downs, the pain in my hip and knee began to decrease and eventually disappeared.

DECREASING THE PAIN OF CHANGE

Change is a lot like running. You can't just get on the treadmill, turn on the Super Nintendo, and go. There is a preliminary warm-up process that makes all the difference in the world in the pain level of change. Some of us are "get it done" kinds of people, and we want to make large, sweeping change immediately—just like I wanted to be able to run without pain and without doing warm-up and cool-down exercises. But rushing into change will almost always cause great chaos.

THE FAST WAY OR THE RIGHT WAY

I have learned that the process of change—rather than change itself—can be destructive if not managed effectively. Let me tell you about one of the times my pastor and our staff learned this lesson, the hard way.

We all know stories of churches that have tried to make major changes without good processes and have caused more pain than gain. I remember the first time we tried to go to two weekend services in the church where I serve. We talked about it as a staff and simply decided that because of the demands of growth, it made sense to add another service. We made a decision on Tuesday, the senior pastor left for vacation on Thursday, and one of the assistant pastors made the announcement the next Sunday morning as a done deal.

The church had never had more than one morning service in its many years of existence. The people, an average attendance of 500 (including children and students) were not about to change that easily. Within the next few days there was a petition drive with over one hundred names on the list. That meant 20 percent of the people had signed the petition—35 percent of the adults. They wanted to meet and find out what was going on and why.

There had been no preparation for this kind of change. There had been no vision cast that gave us a focused picture as to why we would make this decision. As I look back, I can hardly imagine that we tried to make such a major change in such a foolish way. We ended up meeting with the congregation and the local board. And we eventually took time to process this idea more completely.

In our meeting with the congregation, people expressed many legitimate and heartfelt needs and concerns: They did not want to have multiple services because they would no longer get to see people with whom they had attended church all of their lives. They were afraid the congregation would split into two churches instead of one united unit. They knew how difficult it would be to double our volunteer staff. It was important that they had a legitimate voice. After all, it would affect their personal family schedules, their places of serving in the church, and which of their friends they would see or not see on any given Sunday.

In that same meeting, the leadership team was able to share with the people the demands of growth and the need to make room for people who did not yet know Christ. In short, we were able to communicate vision for a greater tomorrow of impacting our community for Christ.

As people began to see and understand why we wanted to make this decision, they were able to accept it more easily. In the days ahead we were able to make a more deliberate and supported decision to move into the two-service format.

Since that time we have changed our format many times. And our people have been able to make each of these adjustments because of better process, better communication, and a better understanding of the purpose.

A PICTURE OF THE FUTURE

As you can learn from this experience at Central Wesleyan, it is of utmost importance that you paint a picture of the preferred future and help people understand why change is necessary if you want them to accept change graciously. Our business administrator talks about an economic principle that goes like this, "Until the price of *not* changing is higher than the price of changing, most people will choose to not change." That is true in the ministry, as well as in business and personal life. We all enjoy being comfortable. Even if our current situation is not best, it is still familiar and comfortable.

For example, in our church some of the feedback we heard went like this, "My wife and I have sat with Fred and Mary for the last ten years at church. What if they go to a different service than we do?" "And all those new people who are coming, one of those new families sat in my favorite pew last week. I don't think I like all this change."

What are the warm-up exercises for initiating successful change? As demonstrated in our example, it is necessary to go through the preliminaries of casting vision clearly and powerfully, allowing time for processing, casting more vision, telling stories of success, giving people opportunities to ask questions, and inviting people to help shape the journey. When these things happen, people begin to own the change and are often willing to make personal sacrifices to see the change implemented.

We must recognize that almost all change involves grief for someone. I encourage you to find ways to acknowledge that grief more effectively. Better communication, improved processes, and greater openness and vulnerability will help you deal with the grief of change more graciously. Processing that grief does not compromise the change. It simply makes the journey easier for those affected. In time, you will create a culture in which people expect change and learn to accept it rather than resist it.

Ways you might involve people in major change include focus groups, surveys, personal testimonies, time at staff meetings, time at board meetings, meetings with key lay leaders, meetings with people who are most directly affected, and creating a variety of printed materials that answer frequently asked questions and cast the vision for this change.

Keep in mind that people will embrace what they have a sense of mission about. When people see they are going to be part of something that has eternal value, something that will make a difference, they will embrace change more readily. It's when they have a sense that this change is just for someone's ease or comfort—or is just to be trendy—that they will resist more vehemently.

A JOURNEY OF CHANGE

A number of years ago I decided it would be best if our adult choir sang all of their music from memory. I had seen a couple of choirs do this and was amazed at how much more eye contact they had with the audience, how much more engaged they were in worship, and how much more effective their overall ministry was. I knew this would be a major challenge for our choir who had never done anything like this. I decided it would be much better to take them on a journey of change rather than simply make an announcement of change.

First, I picked two songs we had done the year before and included them in our selections for the coming year. The choir had liked these particular songs and performed them well. After rehearsing those songs for a couple of weeks, I asked the choir in rehearsal one night to put their music down and try to sing one of the songs from memory, just for fun. After a few stumbles, they made it the whole way through, and everyone clapped and thought it was fun. A couple of weeks later, we sang that song in the service from memory. The congregation was blessed, and the choir felt good about that accomplishment. We did the same with the other song. The next year we did that a few more times.

The third year I made a speech to the choir about how much more effective their ministry was when they were not looking down at their music and how much more they seemed to worship the Lord. I told them that next year I was planning to ask them to do all of their music from memory. I told them I would provide tools to make that easier: printed music for all of the songs at least three months in advance and rehearsal tapes so they could practice on their own.

Two or three people said, "I can't do that," and they dropped out of choir. One lady, who was in her early 50s, wrote me a letter and said she thought this was more than she could do but she would give it a try. The majority of the choir saw the value, had experienced a taste of it, and decided to go for it. We have done all of our music from memory ever since. Incidentally, the lady who sent me the letter sent another letter at the end of the first year of memorized music. In the second letter, she expressed appreciation for challenging her to do something she never believed she could do. She felt great having accomplished such a challenging task.

THE PROCESS OF CHANGE

As if all that is not enough, now comes the really hard part. All of this discussion has, no doubt, stimulated some fun, scary, and challenging images as you have reflected on how you might take this kind of bold step in your local church. But it is the *how* that we'll address now—how to develop a clear process of change when you find God moving you into new ventures.

DETERMINE KEY PLAYERS AND STAKEHOLDERS

Your first step will be to identify key players who should be included early in the process. This probably includes a variety of people depending on your local situation. In most cases it will include the senior pastor, some staff members, some board members or elders, as well as some stakeholders, whom I would define as people who have invested heavily in the ministry of this church. That investment is more than financial. It includes people who have served and have given of themselves and their resources to help get the church where it is today. Other stakeholders might represent key participants in specialized demographics, such as young adults, senior adults, men, women, new people, seasoned veterans, blue-collar workers, professionals, single adults, parents, grandparents, etc. It is helpful to get a broad representation of people to be part of this team. Their diversity will prove valuable.

As you compose your group, you'll want to consider all of the issues we've discussed to this point regarding personality tests (DISC, Myers/Briggs, and Personality Dynamic Profile [PDP]) and spiritual gifts tests. As we mentioned in chapters six and seven, these tests can be useful in evaluating and placing leadership into roles for which they are best suited. They also can help increase understanding among team members.

It is helpful to be sure a group is composed of people with a broad representation of gifts. Sometimes leaders will recruit a group of people who think the same, are gifted similarly, and act in similar ways. Instead, God's representation of many gifts within the body of Christ shows us that a healthy group is one that brings together people who are gifted differently to complement each other—and to compensate for each other's weaknesses.

Once you've identified your group, you might try to schedule a *Charette*—a French word that has come to describe a short, one-day planning session that involves teams of participants with diverse skills working together on one well-defined task.

ESTABLISH A PRAYER TEAM

The next step is to do what we suggested back in chapter five: establish a prayer team with prayer partners for each participant. Make it a non-negotiable requirement that every member of the team recruit people to serve as prayer partners for them during the process. Ask everyone to turn in that list of names, and then create an e-mail or postal mailing list for that group. Have someone who is passionate about prayer serve as prayer coordinator and send regular reports of answers to prayer, prayer requests, items coming up for discussion, current challenges, etc. Make sure there is regular and effective communication with all of the prayer partners and effective affirmation of their important ministry.

IDENTIFY THE TOOLS YOU WILL NEED

Third, you'll want to identify tools you may need for this process. Some suggestions for typical change situations are—

Interview Forms and Formats. As a part of the research process, you may need to interview people from the community, other churches, other organizations, or constituents within your own congregation. Well-planned interview forms will help standardize the collection of information to make tabulation and interpretation of data go smoothly.

Surveys. Sometimes it is helpful to formally gather data and information from your congregation. This can be done through a formal survey. A number of organizations can assist you with this process. One organization I have worked with is J. David Schmidt and Associates in Wheaton, Illinois. They can assist in crafting questions, interpreting data, and applying results to an organization's planning process.

Community Documents and Data. Often a local Chamber of Commerce or community planning commission will have data available about housing trends, average income, economic trends, demographics, and a variety of other statistics that would be of help to you in looking to the future. These documents can give you a better understanding of the people groups in your local community.

Recommended Books about Change or Planning Processes. You may want to create a recommended reading list for planning team members. This could include both books on the subject of change and books about specific kinds of ministry you are seeking to launch. One of the best books I have read on change is *How To Change Your Church (Without Killing It),* by Alan Nelson and Gene Appel.[1]

Outside Counsel. At times it is necessary to have an outside person help you walk through the process, especially if this is the first time you have undertaken a change of this magnitude. An unbiased third party who is not involved in the content of the change can serve as a facilitator to smooth out the process. So your challenge here would be to identify a professional consultant or a person who is a gifted facilitator and does this type of leadership in his or her vocation to help with meetings, gathering data, and managing emotions objectively. Several Christian firms are set up to help in this way.

Success Stories. It also may be helpful to have people share with your group what this type of journey was like at their church or organization. Testimonials can serve as encouragement and help put things into perspective, especially when you get hung up in some area.

CREATE A TIMELINE

Early in the process it is crucial to outline a general timeline. Although it may change many times during the journey, it is worthwhile to begin by setting targets and giving people a picture of what they are committing to.

Here are some questions you may want to consider as you draft your initial timeline:

- When do we begin?

- How long do we allow for the formation of our ministry planning team, and who will be responsible for recruiting this team?

- Do the people who serve on this team need to be approved by the governing body?

- How long do we allow for the input from the congregation, stakeholders and key leaders?

- How long do we allow for the digesting process? (This will include compiling, interpreting, and suggesting application of data.)

- How long do we allow for the recommended design process of applying gathered data to a specific design for future programming?

- How long do we allow for the public communication process? (We'll cover this step more completely in a few moments.)

- How long do we allow for the implementation process? (Some changes may need immediate implementation, but others need to have a longer process and a greater involvement from the congregation.)

- How will we measure success?

COMMUNICATE

Once you have a design and a timeline in place, it is imperative that you put a lot of effort into how this gets publicly communicated. There will be technical pieces of the whole picture that do not need to be shared with everyone. But there also will be critical pieces that involve change for large numbers of people that will need to be carefully and thoughtfully communicated. It would be best to establish a communication team of people whose primary responsibility is to get the message out in formal and informal ways, all under the leadership of the planning team chairperson.

Before we get into the public communication of the plan, let's consider the internal communications necessary. Foundational to the whole planning, implementation, and communication process is that the senior pastor is in full support. It is best if the senior pastor is the one who is passionately leading the charge and is able to preach with deep passion about this vision and direction.

The staff, too, will be greatly affected by most changes and new ways of doing church. So be sure to communicate clearly and often with them, offering them participation in the journey along the way.

Likewise, it is vital that the lay leadership be involved in the shaping, developing, and communication. Depending on the church, this may be the board of elders, the local board of administration, the board of deacons, etc. This group must have deep ownership if the plan is to have long-term impact.

Once the internal leaders are in the communication loop, here are some ways to take the message public to the whole organization or congregation. You might use technical tools such as PowerPoint presentations or pre-produced videos.

You might choose printed sources such as articles in the church newsletter, bulletin, or church Web site. Perhaps you can plan two or three issues of your church newsletter dedicated to promoting and explaining this new plan. Also, the church's Web site can be used to support this plan. As we mentioned earlier, providing links for people to give you honest feedback and encouragement helps them feel both heard and well served. Other printed handouts could be as simple as a business-card-sized handout that reminds people to pray or as sophisticated as a four-color brochure that gives a detailed description of the church's vision and ministry plan with a tear-off question and comment portion to be placed in the offering plate.

You might choose personal testimonies to communicate the vision in public worship services, staff meetings, and board meetings. There is great power in a personal testimony. That is why Michael Jordan and Tiger Woods get paid so much money to endorse lines of products. Advertisers know that if significant people endorse or promote a product, others will buy on the basis of the person's testimony. In spiritual matters when we hear a testimony of how God used someone to lead another person to faith in Christ, we are encouraged to believe God could use us as well. When we hear someone tell of how God moved them to a place of obedience in tithing, we come to believe God could do the same in our lives.

If one group is going to be especially affected, you might hold smaller focus groups to allow people to process the change in an interactive way in a non-threatening, non-public setting.

To communicate a basic message to the broadest constituency within your church, you might post banners and posters in the church lobby, worship center, and classrooms. Or you might create posters for hallways, entrance doors, or bulletin boards. Seeing these bigger-than-life depictions of a clear vision or change in direction can be a profitable way of reminding people about the direction the church is moving. Similarly, key chains or other take-home items can serve as reminders for people to pray, to participate, and to engage in this new approach to ministry. We handed out small pieces of jigsaw puzzles to all of our people on a Sunday when the pastor preached about discovering your spiritual gifts and how you fit into the kingdom of God. The puzzle piece was a reminder to all of us that we are part of the bigger picture and that God wants to use us to complete His picture.

CREATE METHODS OF EVALUATION

Even before initiating change, it is useful to create an evaluation component of the project. Many times we are guilty of making major changes but not doing an effective job of evaluation after the initiative is completed. Tools for evaluation may include some of the following:

Surveys. By surveying the people affected by these changes a few months after the fact, you will learn a great deal about their impact. You will begin to see whether the changes are causing the church to move in the right direction.

Web Site Feedback. Create a simple way for people to click on a link and send an e-mail with their thoughts about an issue. Make sure you monitor that feedback on a regular basis. Always acknowledge receipt of the feedback without agreeing or disagreeing (or worse, arguing) with the content.

Numerical Measurements. What has been the result numerically? Sometimes we go through what is known as a change valley, or a dip in emotions or numbers during the process of change. This is normal. A commonly used model for interpreting change, which I learned from Dr. Keith Drury, makes sense of this phenomenon. The Change

Valley illustrates that the equilibrium established after the turbulence of change will bring us to a greater height than before.

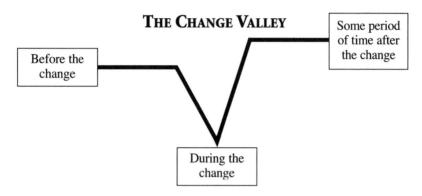

Make sure you allow enough time to pass to give a genuine evaluation of the numbers. It is not uncommon to see a dip in the numbers when a change is implemented. Don't make a hasty, reactive response to a loss of numbers that may be part of the change valley and may actually lead to increased growth.

Attendance. That said, though, make sure you are paying attention to attendance patterns. Can you identify a clear cause-and-effect relationship between attendance and the changes you have made? Have new patterns developed that have been impacted by change of schedule, change of program offerings, season of the year, new facilities, etc.? Are new people coming? It is important that we measure the impact of changes on reaching new people. If all we have done is shuffle around people who were already coming, the changes may not have been as successful as we had hoped. Keep building on the things that are reaching new people and let some of the other things go by the wayside.

Number of People Demonstrating the Desired Behaviors (such as participating in a small group, sharing their faith, inviting nonchurched people to church). If the ministry plan that you have adopted has specific desired behaviors, you should be able to see measurable results in those areas. In our church we wanted to see a greater number of people participate in small groups. As a result, we created a strategy to make that happen. We went from 700 to over 2000 in small groups in a relatively short time. This gave us a good measurement of change in desired behaviors.

Number of People Who Left (make sure this is not just rumor from some who are complaining). This can be emotional and difficult to measure. It is hard to know when someone has come and left if they never got plugged in. It is also difficult to know why people leave. Their leaving may or may not have anything to do with the changes you made. We have had people leave our church because they moved to a new neighborhood and wanted to try the closest church. Some have left because of job transfers. Some have left because the church was getting too large. Others have left because of being negatively affected by the changes that were made. Make sure you track this and follow up the best way you can. We send people an exit questionnaire to ask if they would be willing to share with us what their experience was like at our church and why they left. We have been able to learn many helpful things through this feedback.

Congregational morale. Do you see a positive response from many in the congregation? Don't let those who express frustration blind you to those who are experiencing new life and new purpose. Do you have a sense that the people of the congregation have a renewed purpose and focus? Do they see themselves as serving the Lord with renewed energy and passion?

Are you hearing stories of how God has used someone in new and exciting ways? We created a link on our Web site called stories.org and asked people to send us their experiences with a new ministry. We got back many stories of how God was using the people of the church at home, at work, and in their neighborhoods. You could place a card in the pews at church and ask people to write a story or experience they have had about how God has used them in a new way related to the change.

Staff morale. Have the changes that have been made served as an encouragement to the staff? Are they leading with a greater sense of purpose and direction? Do they seem more energized? If they are functioning with a clear vision and in the areas of their gifting, passion, and anointing, you will undoubtedly see new levels of power and effectiveness in their lives and in their ministries. Meaningful one-on-one conversations are good and healthy ways to help evaluate this area.

PLAN A CELEBRATION

A final key to making the change process a positive experience is to plan ways to celebrate the implementation of this new plan. Have a church party. Do something to associate this new vision and new direction with great joy, celebration, and camaraderie. Let there be a spirit of teamwork among the staff and congregation as you launch into this new ministry. Let someone with the gift of partying lead the charge on this event. Make a big deal out of it.

Change—especially change initiated by a clear vision, prayerfully established and supported, and wisely implemented—can be a very big deal in the body of Christ. It can allow and equip each member of our churches and organizations to fulfill the Great Commission with more success and more vitality than we'd ever thought possible. It is worthy of great celebration.

So go through the process. Endure the risk. Work through the pain. Then look back and see what God is doing in and through you. You know, if the changes we initiate are reaching new people with the message of Jesus Christ, there's already a party going on in heaven. So let's join in. Let's celebrate our God-given clear vision— and let's throw a party.

SEEING THE FUTURE

1. Take few minutes to pray, asking God to speak to you about what you have just read in this chapter. Are there things He wants to speak to you about, things He wants to "burn into your heart," things He wants you to act upon?

2. What word best describes your church's approach to change: welcoming, resistant, tolerant, expectant, or fearful?

3. Name the two or three most recent changes you have experienced. How did you manage them? What lessons could be learned from those experiences that might help you manage future changes?

4. What changes do you anticipate making in the next year? Name the key stakeholders who can assist with this process.

AFTERWORD

———⟊⟊⟊———

J ust a few months ago, our local church was going through a time of spiritual malaise that some described as a season of "complaint management" instead of "mission accomplishment." A member of our management team suggested we participate in an intense spiritual growth initiative with the vision of helping our congregation unite around a clear and common theme, study a prescribed set of materials, and process spiritual truth as a congregation as well as in small groups. The goal was gaining a new level of spiritual energy for our entire local church.

As I have seen and participated in this initiative, it occurred to me that the thesis and principles of this book were playing out right before my eyes. It has been exciting and motivating to see the real-life results of a ministry that has gone through the process of clarifying vision.

Let me share the process with you, as this may help translate all of the theory we've been discussing into real life application.

VISION CASTING

When the idea for this program came to our attention, the senior pastor began the process of casting vision for it. He met with the church staff, provided written materials, and shared testimonials about how others had found this to be a positive experience. He initiated extended prayer around this ministry and met with our local board of administration (the elected lay leadership in our church) to cast the vision. Then he began dividing responsibilities to deepen our individual ownership through participation.

We began to visualize pictures of what success could look like if this went well. The more we came together, the more united our thoughts and hearts became, and the more motivated we were to dig deeper into this powerful opportunity.

As this unfolded it was awesome to see people catch the vision, eagerly pursue their roles in bringing that picture to fruition, endure challenges, create solutions, and experience freedom to move ahead. Because the pastor made the destination and the values to get there clear, we have experienced an increase in positive team interactions—even among sub-teams. The clarity of purpose, the clarity of vision, and the clarity of responsibility has been powerful and has resulted in a synergistic effort that has already borne fruit.

TEAM BUILDING

Once the whole group had owned the vision, we divided into sub-teams. One team was focused on planning the worship services to support the overall themes of this eight-week initiative. Another team was focused on forming small groups to address the topics of this eight-week initiative. This involved recruiting, training, motivating, and resourcing small group leaders. It also involved the huge task of matching people into small groups where they would experience affinity with others. This was a huge job requiring administrative gifts and people gifts.

Another team was focused on communication, promotion, and advertising. This team knew exactly what to promote and advertise because they had a clear picture of the vision for an eventual outcome. Another team was responsible for preparing dramas to communicate the themes in creative ways.

Two teams focused on making the initiative fit students: one for middle school and high school students, another for preschool and grade school children. They maintained the same themes and emphases, but adapted them to be age appropriate.

THE FRUIT OF SUCCESS

A focused vision clearly communicated made this initiative a success. Each staff member knew what the overall picture of success looked like. All of them understood their roles well enough to offer encouragement and support to others. We refocused our budget to reflect this initiative and supported it financially. (The tradeoff was that some other things were not being done while this initiative was ongoing. This was accomplished with little or no hassle because the staff and the people believed in this vision.)

All of them knew the vision, knew their roles within that vision, and were focused on and moving in the same direction. That unity and clear understanding was synergistically powerful. The staff was motivated and energized. The people of the congregation were influenced to take tangible steps toward spiritual maturity.

Some examples of that fruit from this initiative are—

• A number of individuals made first-time commitments to Jesus Christ.

• More people expressed a desire to be baptized.

• A record number of people committed to being part of a small group ministry, and we are receiving positive reports about the impact small groups are having in the lives of the participants.

• More people memorized Scripture.

• More people expressed interest in discovering their spiritual gifts and getting involved in service.

• Consumer complaints diminished as people deeply engaged in what God wanted to do in their lives.

• A higher level of spiritual and emotional energy was evident among the staff, the lay leadership, and the congregation at large.

• More people of the church reached out and built redemptive relationships with those outside the church.

• We saw greater focus, purpose and power in our public worship services.

• Tired people became invigorated and strengthened to re-engage in ministry with increased effectiveness.

This kind of result cannot happen when there is a lack of clarity with the leadership of the church or with the people of the church. Let me emphasize that this is not a promotion for any particular initiative but rather an illustration of how great the impact is when we have before us a crystal clear vision, fully recognize the values that drive us, and clearly understand the role we have to fulfill in seeing that vision come into being.

ENVISIONING YOUR CLEAR SUCCESS

I believe God wants to accomplish the same kind of success in His vision for your ministry and your church. Let me encourage you to go after it. Get serious with God in prayer. Get a group of committed people who will fast and pray and seek God's face with you. Get a clear picture of what you sense God directing you to do, and then pursue it with reckless abandon.

Don't go it alone. Make sure you have a team of people including key staff and lay leaders who affirm that this is, in fact, from the Lord. Make sure you have someone outside your church involved who can be objective and help you through difficult, emotional times. God will honor your humble obedience, your faith, and your deep desire to see His Kingdom increased.

You will face challenges you have never faced. You will encounter resistance. But you also will see victories you've never seen. You will experience great camaraderie. You will see people step up in ways you never imagined. People will discover passions and gifts they never knew they had. You will see God's hand at work in ways you've not seen before. I encourage you to take a step of faith and see where God takes you as you venture into new territory in the name of Jesus Christ.

Let me close with this prayer for you:

Father,

I pray in Jesus' name that You will take the thoughts that have been shared in this book and use them in the life of the person who is reading it. May it serve as a tool that causes him or her to seek Your face and to seek Your plans and desires for each local church.

Father, I believe the local church truly is the hope of the world. We stand on Your Word that says the gates of hell will not prevail against Your church. Please help us trust You and walk with You in humble obedience. May we be the leaders who seek to submit ourselves to You to be used by You in any way You choose, even if that means great personal sacrifice.

We want Your name to be blessed and made famous by the efforts we offer in the name of Jesus Christ, the Head of the church.

In Jesus' name,

Amen.

APPENDIX A

—〰—

RECOMMENDED READING

ORGANIZATIONAL LEADERSHIP

The 17 Indisputable Laws of Leadership, by John Maxwell, Thomas Nelson Publishers, Nashville, Tenn., 2001.

The 21 Irrefutable Laws of Leadership, by John Maxwell, Thomas Nelson Publishers, Nashville, Tenn., 1998.

Built to Last, by James C. Collins and Jerry I. Porras, Harper Business, New York, 1994.

Courageous Leadership, by Bill Hybels, Zondervan Publishing, Grand Rapids, Mich., 2002.

Good to Great, by James Collins, Harper Business, New York, 2001.

If You Want to Walk on Water You've Got to Get Out of the Boat, by John Ortberg, Zondervan Publishing, Grand Rapids, Mich., 2001.

Lead On, by Wayne Schmidt, Wesleyan Publishing House, Indianapolis, Ind., 2003.

Leadership and the One Minute Manager, by Ken Blanchard, and Patricia and Drea Zigarmi, William Morrow and Company, Inc., New York, 1985.

Thinking for a Change, by John C. Maxwell, Warner Books, New York, 2003.

PERSONAL LEADERSHIP AND DEVELOPMENT

Choosing to Cheat, by Andy Stanley, Thomas Nelson Publishers, Nashville, Tenn., 2002.

Living the Life You Were Meant to Live, by Tom Patterson, Thomas Nelson Publishers, Nashville, Tenn., 1998.

Pastors at Greater Risk, by H.B. London and Neil Wiseman, Regal Books, Ventura, Calif., 2003.

Visioneering, by Andy Stanley, Multnomah Publishers, Sisters, Ore., 1999.

CHANGE MANAGEMENT AND PROCESS

How to Change Your Church (Without Killing It), by Alan Nelson and Gene Appel, W Publishing, 2000.

The Next Step, by Bob Sorrell, Baxter Press, Inc., 2001.

TEAM DEVELOPMENT

The Five Dysfunctions of a Team, by Patrick Lencioni, Jossey-Bass, San Francisco, 2002.

PHILOSOPHICAL APPROACH TO MINISTRY

The Church of Irresistible Influence, by Robert Lewis with Rob Wilkins, Zondervan Publishing, Grand Rapids, Mich., 2001.

The Present Future, by Reggie McNeal, Jossey-Bass, San Francisco, 2003.

Worship Evangelism, by Sally Morgenthaler, Zondervan Publishing House, Grand Rapids, Mich., 1995.

Appendix B

—ллл—

Suggested Personality and Spiritual Gift Tests

Passion and Heart Exercise

This is an exercise designed to assist you in evaluating where you sense the anointing of the Lord in your life. It will assist you in identifying those places, times, events, ministries, etc., for which the Lord has anointed you. It will help you identify passions God has given you and will show you some ways He wants to use those passions in your life and ministry. For further information about this process contact:

Team Development, Inc.

Don Cousins

932 Chelsea Court

Holland, Mich. 49423

616.396.9625

PERSONALITY TEST

The PDP test is designed to assist in identifying how a person is naturally wired, compared to the environment he or she is working in. It also measures how much energy is being expended to act in ways outside the natural wiring. For more information contact:

PDP Inc.

719-687-6074

pdpinc@aol.com

www.pdpnet.com

SPIRITUAL GIFT TESTS AVAILABLE ON THE INTERNET

Spiritual Gifts Discovery Tool, http://www.cforc.com/sgifts.html

A relatively simple and quick test that can taken online or offline. It will help identify spiritual gifts that are found in 1 Corinthians 12, Romans 12, and Ephesians 4 as well as gifts such as music, craftsmanship, intercessory prayer, and wisdom.

Team Ministry Spiritual Gifts Analysis, http://www.church-growth.org/cgi-cg/gifts.cgi

At this site you can do a free individual gifts assessment, or you can do a group evaluation for a fee.

Cyberspace Ministry Spiritual Gifts Assessment, http://www.tag-net.org/cyberspace/Services/Gifts/Eng/eng-gift.html

This is a test taken online and submitted via e-mail for scoring and evaluation. Cyberspace Ministry will send you an assessment via e-mail that will assist in identifying and deploying your spiritual gifts.

BBC Spiritual Gifts Assessment, http://www.bethany-ca.edu/mygifts/
This is a spiritual gifts test connected with Bethany Bible College
in Sussex, New Brunswick, Canada.

SPIRITUAL GIFT TESTS AVAILABLE IN PRINT

Modified Heights Spiritual Gifts Survey by Paul R. Ford

ChurchSmart Resources

3830 Ohio Ave.

Saint Charles, IL 60174

This gifts inventory helps you determine how you may be gifted.
Your gifts not only define the ministry roles in which you could
serve, but also reveal how you will serve, teach, or lead.

Uniquely You In Christ, by Mels Carbonell, Ph.D.

Uniquely You

P.O. Box 490

Blue Ridge, GA 30513

This booklet is designed to assist you in discovering your spiritual gifts, talents, interests, and passions.

Haugk Spiritual Gifts Inventory, used in conjunction with
*Discovering God's Vision for Your Life—You and Your Spiritual
Gifts,* by Kenneth C. Haugk.

Tebunah Ministries

7053 Lindell Blvd.

St. Louis, MO 63130

These two resources are part of a complete set of integrated resources for use in congregations to help people discover, develop, and deploy their spiritual gifts.

Gifts of Grace—Discovering and Using Your Spiritual Gifts by Larry Garner and Tony Martin.

Baptist Book Store

Jackson, MS 39201

This resource brings balance based on the biblical teachings concerning grace gifts (spiritual gifts) and their operation on the church. It includes a spiritual gifts test.

The Spiritual Gifts Inventory with DISC Personality Overview, by The Institute for Motivational Living, Inc.

3307 Wilmington Road

P.O. Box 925

New Castle, PA 16103

This resource will assist a follower of Christ to understand how to be involved in the area of their gifting, as well as understand one's self and others to work in harmony with the other members of the body.

Spiritual Gifts Inventory (Team Ministry) by Larry Gilbert

Ephesians Four Ministries

Church Growth Institute P.O. Box 7

Elkton, MD 21922

Discover your spiritual gifts with this easy-to-use resource.

NOTES

—⟋⟍—

INTRODUCTION

1. Andy Stanley, *The Next Generation Leader,* Multnomah Publishing House, Sisters, Ore., 2003, p. 68.

CHAPTER ONE

1. George Barna. *The Barna Update*, (May 2004), The Barna Group, 1957 Eastman Ave. Suite B, Ventura, CA 93003.

2. Robert Lewis with Rob Wilkins, *The Church of Irresistible Influence,* Zondervan Publishing House, Grand Rapids, Mich., 2001, p. 55.

3. L. Richards. *Every Man in the Bible*, Thomas Nelson Publishers, Nashville, Tenn., 1999 (Libronix Digital Library System).

CHAPTER TWO

1. George Barna. *The Barna Update,* (December 17, 2001), The Barna Group, 1957 Eastman Ave. Suite B, Ventura, CA 93003.

2. Charles Chaney, *Church Planting at the End of the Twentieth Century*, Tyndale House Publishers, Wheaton, Ill., 1998, p. 60.

CHAPTER THREE

1. Andy Stanley, *Choosing to Cheat*, Thomas Nelson Publishers, Nashville, Tenn., 2002, p. 8.

2. Bill Hybels, *Courageous Leadership,* Zondervan Publishing House, Grand Rapids, Mich., 2002, p. 236.

CHAPTER FIVE

1. Jim Cymbala. *Fresh Wind, Fresh Fire,* Zondervan Publishing House, Grand Rapids, Mich., 1997, pp. 63–65.

2. Ibid.

CHAPTER SIX

1. While there may be some debate about this, I suspect that these lists are not intended to be all-inclusive. For example, many people are specially gifted as prayer intercessors, while others are specially gifted to use the arts to honor God.

2. For more detail about the SHAPE curriculum, check out *Developing Your SHAPE to Serve Others* by Brett Eastman at www.pastors.com.

CHAPTER SEVEN

1. Jim Collins, *Good to Great*, Harper Business, New York, 2001, p. 41.

2. For more information on the PDP test, see Appendix B.

CHAPTER EIGHT

1. Bill Hybels, *Courageous Leadership,* Zondervan Publishing House, Grand Rapids, Mich., 2002, p. 236.

CHAPTER NINE

1. See Appendix A for more suggestions on recommended reading in the area of change and other subjects we've covered in this book.

For further information or consulting services, contact:

Jack Lynn

www.jacklynn.org

916 Pioneer Ave.

Holland, MI 49423

Your feedback is welcome at:

Clearvision@jacklynn.org

The Leading Pastor Series offers solutions to contemporary issues facing pastors and church leaders. This relevant and practical series provides guidance from leading pastors with proven leadership ability.

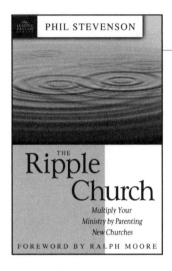

PHIL STEVENSON

The Ripple Church

Multiply Your Ministry
by Parenting New Churches

By Phil Stevenson

The Ripple Church will inspire you to become involved in church planting and provide practical steps for planting churches from existing congregations.

BKBF16 $12.99
Order Online: 0898272718

As senior pastor, **Phil Stevenson** led two of his congregations in the parenting of seven new churches. He is now a senior consultant and coach at New Church Specialties, an organization that assists in the starting and strengthening of churches worldwide.

wesleyan
publishing
house

igniting a passion for God in all of life!

To order, call: 800.4 WESLEY (800.493.7539)
or visit: www.wesleyan.org/wph

Ministry Momentum

How to Get It, Keep It, and Use It in Your Church

By Wayne Schmidt

Join Wayne Schmidt as he examines the Old Testament leadership style of Joshua to identify the origin of spiritual momentum. Learn about the eight *Momentum Builders* and *Momentum Busters* that make this book highly practical for every spiritual leader.

BKBF52 $12.99
Order Online: 0898272807

Lead On

Why Churches Stall and How Leaders Get Them Going

By Wayne Schmidt
Foreword by Bill Hybels

Lead On explains how leaders can use the "slow times" God provides to refocus on the mission, identify God's direction for their ministry, and position the church for growth.

BKBC14 $12.99
Order Online: 0898272610

Wayne Schmidt has served as pastor at Kentwood Community Church in Kentwood, Michigan, since its inception in 1979. From a small care groups, KCC has grown into a vibrant congregation that averages more than 2,500 in weekend worship services and is instrumental in leading more than 100 adults to Christ each year.

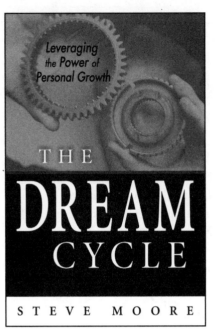

The Dream Cycle

Leveraging the Power of Personal Growth

By Steve Moore

Steve Moore has a passion to see leaders, and the organizations they lead, realize their potential and maximize effectiveness. *The Dream Cycle* offers a repeatable model of personal learning that enables leaders to leverage the power of personal growth, turning God-given vision into reality. Provide your church leaders and board members with *The Dream Cycle* and encourage them to fulfill their God-given dreams!

BKBF51 $14.99
Order Online: 0898272777

Steve Moore has served as a local church pastor and mission executive, most recently with Keep Growing, Inc. Steve's heart for the world and skill for developing leaders has taken him to more than 40 nations in 17 years of active ministry.

wesleyan
publishing
house

igniting a passion for God in all of life!

To order, call: 800.4 WESLEY (800.493.7539)
or visit: www.wesleyan.org/wph